Steps to Success

Practical advice for entrepreneurs based on interviews with Canadian and American business luminaries

Avi Rosen
with Gabrielle Bauer

KENDALL/HUNT PUBLISHING COMPANY
4050 Westmark Drive   Dubuque, Iowa 52002

Copyright Respect is a Two-Way Street!

As an educator, I recognize the need to copy parts of educational materials from time to time. You may reproduce parts of this book, up to 100 copies, via any medium without permission from the author *provided that you do not make a profit from it.*

I ask that you respect my rights by using the following guidelines when copying parts of this book: use *quality soft coloured paper*, keep pages *straight*, and do not omit the *book title and my name* from then. Be honest with people as to the source of these ideas, and encourage sales of the book when you can.

For information on a personalized, in-house seminar on "Steps to Success," contact:

Avi Rosen and Associates
32 Covewood Street
North York, Ontario
M2M 2Z1
Tel. (416) 410-1314
Fax (416) 221-7280

Copyright © 1996 by Avi Rosen

ISBN 0-7872-1624-0

All right reserved. No part of this publication may be reproduced, stored in a retrieval system, or transmitted, in any form or by any means, electronic, mechanical, photocopying, recording, or otherwise, without the prior written permission of the copyright owner.

Printed in the United States of America

10 9 8 7 6 5 4 3 2 1

Dedication

To my mother, Ida
and my sons,
Larry, Michael and Allan

STEPS TO SUCCESS

"Being the best at what you do leads to a certain inner confidence that customers, staff and employees can feel. Confidence comes after accomplishment, not before it. The only way to build confidence is by doing."

Peter Oliver
Owner, Oliver's Restaurants

"I enjoy talking about my failures, because I and my staff have gotten our best laughs from them, and besides, they've all been learning experiences."

Jerry Goodis
Advertising Spokesman

"Marketing communicates what you have to offer to your customer that compels them to desire you over your competitors—and for their self-serving reasons, not yours."

Jo Stumpf
Marketing Expert

"As it relates to the concept of no hassle, attitude can be summed up by the sentence, 'I am going to make it as easy as possible for you to do business with me.'"

Jerry Wilson
Sales and Management Trainer

"Yes, my theory is to do the opposite. Everything in our society is geared to make you look average, so doing the opposite allows you to be above average. Certainly it has made all the difference for me and my business."

Harilyn Jennings
Leading Real Estate Salesperson

"These days, service is the name of the game. And if we can come up with a useful and original service that's somehow related to our products, we get noticed."

Alex Tilley
Owner of Tilley Endurables

"Instead of being so focused on how the other person can be of use to you, find out how you can be of use to them."

Bob Burg
Motivational Lecturer

Contents

Avi Rosen vii
About the Interviewees and Authors ix
Introduction xiii

1 First Steps
   The Entrepreneurial Spirit 1

2 Marketing
   The Method Behind the Mystery 33

3 Organization
   The Well-Oiled Machine 57

4 Creative Thinking
   The Power of Ideas 79

5 Communication
   The Art of Connecting 99

6 Steps Ahead
   Toward a Successful Future 125

Further Steps 149
Excerpts From Letters to Avi Rosen 150
Other Tools 151

AVI ROSEN

His dancing eyes, infectious smile and lilting voice entertain, educate and inspire business people from all walks of life who turn to Avi Rosen for advice and help in achieving their goals. With over 31 years' experience in the corporate and business consulting field, Avi brings a wealth of knowledge and insight to any topic he tackles.

Avi's expertise has been gleaned carefully from the variety of prestigious positions he's held over the years. During that time, he has owned his own real estate brokerage firm, taught in the Business Department at Ryerson University, served as a Board Member of the Toronto Real Estate Board, served as a marketing consultant for Royal LePage, Realty World and Homelife, and he has published articles in various real estate periodicals.

Now a full-time trainer, consultant, writer and speaker, Avi dedicates his efforts to educating those in the business world through various forms of media, including books, newsletters, audio and video tapes and seminar courses. In fact, Avi is one of the most sought-after speakers in the country today, when it comes to dynamic marketing and self-promotion.

Whether he takes the role of motivator, teacher or lecturer, or whether your topic is feasibility, competitor analysis or sales promotion, Avi's advice is on-target and timely. A sense of humour combined with a genuine passion for his work make learning an exciting experience for all his students and readers.

Avi Rosen strives for professional excellence and expects nothing less from you!

Avi Rosen is an internationally known professional speaker. For information on workshops, seminars and keynote addresses, contact:

Avi Rosen and Associates
32 Covewood Street
North York, Ontario M2M 2Z1
Tel. (416) 410-1314
Fax (416) 221-7280

About the Interviewees and Authors

❦ **Bob Burg** has earned wide acclaim as a lecturer on the American motivational speaking circuit, and is the author of the book *Endless Referrals* (McGraw Hill). Excerpts from his cassette-tape learning series are featured daily on the nation's first motivational radio network. Bob's many clients include Marriott, Coldwell Banker and Amway.

❦ **Arthur Fettig** began his speaking career by writing humorous articles and selling them to magazines. This led to a stint as writer/researcher for a professional speaker, a job which inspired him to seek out his own speaking engagements. He was voted top speaker at the World Meeting Planners' Convention in Texas, and is the author of several successful books on lecturing.

❦ **Nancy Friedman,** also known as the Telephone Doctor®, travels around corporate America instructing people on how to be friendlier on the phone. Through Nancy's Enter-Training® programs, thousands of employees have learned how to deliver outstanding customer service on the telephone, and an even larger number of employees have benefitted from her video-based training programs.

❦ **Patricia Fripp** has been active for over ten years as a professional speaker and trainer. In 1983, she received the Council of Peers Award for Excellence, recognized as one of the most prestigious awards for professional speaking, and in 1984 became the first female president of the National Speakers Association. She is the author of the book *Get What You Want*, and has produced numerous audio and video programs.

❦ **Jerry Goodis** has established himself as Canada's best-known advertising spokesman in a stellar career that spans 30 years. His agencies have won more awards per billing dollar than any agency in Canadian history. A dynamic speaker, Jerry has lectured at several major universities in Canada and abroad, has written dozens of articles for international publications, and is the author of two books.

❧ **Brian Grosman** is a leading Canadian practitioner in the field of employment law. He has taught law at McGill University, and was appointed Professor of Law at the University of Saskatchewan, as well as Founding Chairman of the Law Reform Commission of Saskatchewan. He is the author of the book *Corporate Loyalty* (Penguin Books).

❧ **Marilyn Jennings** is one of North America's leading real estate salespeople. She is a member of the Canadian Real Estate Board's "Million Dollar Club," and has received the Board's Award of Merit for nine consecutive years. She has made several national and local television and radio appearances, and has been featured in numerous magazine and newspaper articles.

❧ **Ed Mirvish** is President and Chief Executive Officer of Honest Ed's, the legendary discount store in Toronto's Bloor-Bathurst area. He also owns Toronto's Royal Alexandra Theatre, as well as 6 restaurants adjacent to the venue. His many honours include the Order of Canada, and having his birthday declared Ed Mirvish Day in Toronto.

❧ **Peter Oliver**, a native South African, settled permanently in Canada in 1973 and launched Oliver's Bakery in 1978. This was the start of what was to become an empire of one-of-a-kind eating establishments in the Toronto area. In 1992, Peter co-founded the Stephen Leacock Club, which organizes innovative events to raise funds for children's causes.

❧ **Hugh Rennie** emerged as a business-communications expert from a background of teaching and corporate management. Since 1980, he has focused his attention on public speaking, and has achieved international prominence for his action-packed keynote presentations which incorporate group exercises, role playing and constructive criticism.

About the Interviewees and Authors xi

❦ **Harry Rosen** owns and operates Harry Rosen Inc., a chain of better menswear stores that claims a 22% share of the upscale menswear market. Harry considers community service to be an integral part of his business career, and has had a long association with the Canadian Cancer Society, including a three-year term as Campaign Chairman for the Toronto branch.

❦ **Jo Stumpf** began his career as a real estate salesperson in Chicago. His explosive success in that field prompted him to branch out into the motivational seminar business. Over the next ten years, he went on to establish himself as one of the leading marketing experts in North America. Jo runs his company, Star Performance Seminars, out of Oceanside, California.

❦ **Harold Taylor** is the president of Harold Taylor Time Consultants Inc., a business that specializes in delivering time-management training to the corporate sector. Every year, he gives more than 100 talks, seminars and in-house training courses. He is the author of ten books, hundreds of articles, and a popular video training program.

❦ **Alex Tilley** began his adventure clothing business, Tilley Endurables, with a simple hat. Frustrated in his quest to find a sailing hat that wouldn't blow off, shrink, wear out, or sink, Alex created his own. The hats took off and expanded into a thriving line of travel clothing that has graced the bodies of such celebrities as Pierre Trudeau, Prince Charles and Charlton Heston.

❦ **Peter Urs Bender** left his native Switzerland for Canada in 1967. Though he hardly spoke a word of English when he arrived, today he is one of the country's top speakers, and is touted by the press as the "business presentation guru." He has taught public speaking and business management at Ryerson University, and currently gives seminars to businesspeople all over the world.

❦ **Jerry Wilson** is the president of Jerry Wilson and Associates, which provides sales and management training for associations and private companies. He is the author of the highly successful *Word-of-Mouth Marketing* (John Wiley & Sons) as well as two other books. He has written dozens of feature articles, and his monthly column, "Managing People," appears in 15 regional publications.

❧ ❧ ❧

❧ **Avi Rosen** has been in the corporate and business consulting field for over 31 years. He has owned his own real estate brokerage firm, taught in the business department at Ryerson University, served as a board member on the Toronto Real Estate Board, and published articles in several real-estate journals. Currently, Avi works as a marketing consultant for Royal LePage and conducts his popular "Let's Talk Business" seminars across Canada.

❧ **Gabrielle Bauer** has held in-house editorial positions at Harlequin Enterprises and Thomson Healthcare Communications, and is currently working as a freelance writer and editor in the Toronto area. She is the author of the book *Tokyo, My Everest* (Hounslow Press), which chronicles her experiences in that city.

Introduction

Success. There are as many ways to get there as there are individuals. One thing that all success stories have in common, however, is that they are never created without effort. Winning a lottery is effortless. But winning a lottery is not success. It may provide satisfaction, but not a sense of accomplishment. Success requires both.

This does not mean that the hardest road to success is always the best. There are efficient and inefficient ways to travel the road, and there is no sense in taking a detour if a shortcut is just around the corner.

This book is one such shortcut. Depending on how you use it, it can cut weeks, months, or even years off your road to entrepreneurial success. While the business sections in bookstores are filled with books on how to be a successful manager or businessperson, how to close deals, how to improve your communication skills, etc., this book differs from the others because the advice comes straight from the mouths of Canadian and American entrepreneurial giants—from the horse's mouth, as it were. Just as a pianist is most qualified to teach piano, a successful entrepreneur is most qualified to dispense advice about entrepreneurial success.

The people interviewed for this book are very different from one another. They live in all parts of the continent, and are involved in business ventures ranging from real estate to public speaking to outdoor clothing manufacturing. They are of different ages, backgrounds, and education levels. They all have their own tales of triumph, adversity, and lessons learned along the way. But despite these differences, common threads run through their stories. It is perhaps these common elements that account for the resounding success that each of these individuals has achieved in the business world. They are:

1 **Passion.** In order to have passion, you have to have something to be passionate about. This means you have to find the kind of

business that suits you best and that will excite you over the long term. Some of the interviewees stumbled into their chosen field right off the bat, while others did so only after repeated career changes. But all of them love for what they are doing, and all agree that this love is an essential condition of their success.

2 **Integrity.** True success involves not only making money, but also earning the respect of one's peers, and above all, being able to respect oneself. All the interviewees show genuine caring for their clients. All of them insist on treating them fairly and well. All of them are committed to honesty and integrity in their business practices. And all of them regard community service as an integral part of their work.

3 **Creativity.** Creativity means letting your mind play with all sorts of ideas, including "silly" or "inappropriate" ones. The interviewees are all mental risk takers. They tend to do the opposite of what everybody else is doing, and are not afraid to try outrageous things. Quite often, their most outrageous schemes (which everybody assures them will not work) prove to be their most successful ones.

4 **Perspective.** All the interviewees agree that passion and intensity need to be balanced with a sense of perspective, which includes a sense of humour. They are all able to step back to see the ultimate absurdity of much that goes on in the business world. They have learned (in some cases only after a physical illness gave them a warning) how to deflect, rather than react to, life's stresses and strains.

5 **Vision.** When starting out on their ventures, the interviewees all had a clear idea of what they wanted to achieve in terms of quality, market sector, and business style. Having decided on these things, they were consistent in projecting their images to their clients over the years. While they are sensitive to the winds of change, they do not change their images with every passing breeze. In other words, they have a clear and steady vision of who they are and what they stand for.

The book is divided into six sections, each one containing several steps. Each step is based on the actual experience of one of the interviewees, and is presented with an interview excerpt and an elaboration of the concepts discussed. In all cases, we have aimed to go beyond generalizations and to give specific examples of how the interviewees have put their own business principles into practice. Each of the six sections emphasizes a different aspect of entrepreneurship. The opening section, First Steps, zeroes in on the qualities needed to make it as an entrepreneur, and the final section, Steps Ahead, focuses on how to maintain your success—and sanity—once you've achieved it. The other sections are Marketing, Organization, Creative Thinking, and Communication. There is, of course, an overlap between these categories. Marketing can be creative, communication is a form of marketing, and creativity thrives in a well-organized environment. The choice of section for a particular step is therefore not absolute. Some of the steps fall under the rubric of common sense—or perhaps we should say uncommon sense, since very few businesspeople actually put these "self-evident" points into practice. Other steps will probably surprise you, provoke you, and give you ideas that you might not have run into in the ordinary course of affairs.

A book such as this one is as useful as the reader allows it to be. It is not very productive to read it once and then shelve it. The best thing to do is to use it as a sort of roadmap, a guide to the development of good business sense. We suggest that you read the steps again and again, a few at a time, until you've internalized them. We recommend that you place the book in an accessible spot, perhaps beside your bed, and carefully reread a few of the steps every morning or night. Then, resolve to put those steps into practice in your next business day.

Rather than wishing you good luck in your business ventures, we wish you good ideas, good preparation, and good habits. If you have or develop these things, success is yours for the taking.

Section 1

First Steps

The Entrepreneurial Spirit

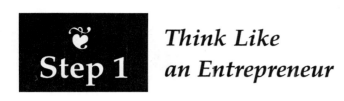

Step 1: Think Like an Entrepreneur

In conversation with Jo Stumpf:

Steps: *"Based on your experience, how should real estate agents be doing business?"*

Stumpf: *"I sold real estate from 1977 through 1981. In that process, I discovered that even though I worked for a real estate company, I really owned my own business and treated it like a business."*

Perhaps you are already working for yourself. On the other hand, you may be working for someone else and contemplating—or actively planning—the move toward self-employment and business ownership. Even if this is the case, the time to start wearing your entrepreneurial hat is right now.

Jo Stumpf's view is that entrepreneurship is a state of mind as much as a state of ownership. While working as an agent for a Chicago real estate company, he quickly realized that success was up to him, not his employer. He then set about devising his own path toward that success.

For instance, he determined that the best use of his time was to go on as many listing presentations as possible and to show as many houses as possible. Everything else was secondary, and could be delegated or deferred. Another part of his strategy consisted of marketing to his inactive clients, whom he saw as a powerful source of referrals. Having formulated these ideas, Jo set about executing them in his own style, which will be discussed further in this book.

The result was that in three years, he went from closing 60 to 120 to 150 transactions.

Even if you are currently working as a salaried, non-commissioned employee, there is room for entrepreneurship in your work. For example, if you are a marketing manager, you can set yourself a personal target of gaining a certain percentage of market share by the end of the year, regardless of your company's objectives. If you are working as a waiter, you can aim for a goal of obtaining X dollars in tips per week. If you are a human resources administrator, you can set yourself the objective of reducing the number of employees who quit or are fired by a certain percentage every year.

No matter where you are working or what you are doing, your place of employment is the perfect laboratory for practising the entrepreneurial spirit.

Step 2: Choose the Right Business For You

In conversation with Ed Mirvish:

Steps: *"What advice would you give to someone just starting out in business?"*

Mirvish: *"Whether it's real estate or students or anyone, the important thing is you have to be interested in and excited about what you're doing. If you can't get excited about it, nothing happens."*

Straightforward as this advice may sound, it is often ignored. A common entrepreneurial mistake is to select a business on the basis of financial prospects alone. When deciding on a type of business, the most important questions to ask yourself are: Am I excited enough about this idea that I won't get discouraged if sales don't take off immediately? Is this an area in which I have some expertise, or potential to develop expertise? Will this business make good use of my intellectual and creative abilities over the years? Can I feel proud of my choice?

A business is much like a personal relationship—it will have peaks and valleys, good times and bad. Choosing the right business is similar to choosing the right spouse: you have to make sure your enthusiasm can survive the difficult times that are sure to come sooner or later.

Ed Mirvish, whose eclectic business ventures may seem puzzling to some, believes that enjoyment is the bottom line. He also believes that people thrive on change, and describes his working day as constantly changing: in the store until noon, in the restaurant from 12:00 to 2:00 p.m., and in the theatre production offices during the later part of the afternoon.

Ed discovered what worked for him—variety—and built his empire on that knowledge. Every budding entrepreneur is unique, and your own preference may be to concentrate on a narrower area. The point is to know yourself—to determine your strengths and limitations, and above all, what turns you on.

Step 3 Plan Ahead For Your Venture

In conversation with Patricia Fripp:

Fripp: *"When I turned up at my NSA [National Speakers' Association] convention, I decided that this was what I wanted to do with my life, even though I was immersed in the hairstyling business at the time."*

Steps: *"And where did you go from there?"*

Fripp: *"I didn't quit my job right away. Instead, I developed a two-year plan to reach my goal, and continued to work in the hairstyling business while carrying out that plan."*

Your business idea... In some cases it hits like a bolt of lightning, and in others it's a slow, almost imperceptible dawning of awareness. One way or another, the day finally comes when you have to roll up your sleeves and map out a plan to make the idea a reality. If you are fortunate enough to be gainfully employed (or self-employed) at this time, you can do what Patricia Fripp did—that is, ease into your new venture while continuing to work at your old job. The obvious advantage of this approach is that you can pay your bills while developing the contacts and skills you will need to make your new enterprise a success.

The disadvantage—that you may be too secure to give your all to the new venture—is less obvious. The way to overcome it is to develop a month-by-month plan that includes timelines for easing out of your old profession. For instance, you can plan to be down to half-time after twelve months, quarter-time after eighteen, and out by the end of two years.

Patricia Fripp discovered her passion for public speaking while doing seminars for a hair-product company. When she came to the realization that speaking was what she wanted to do with her life, she had two years left in a 10-year lease on her own hairstyling company. So she set herself the goal of being a full-time speaker by the time her lease was up. Her step-by-step plan included giving speeches at NSA functions and becoming visible within that organization. Looking back, she believes this strategy "cut 10 years off her learning curve." In fact, she became president of the NSA, and was able to retire from the hairstyling business ahead of plan.

Step 4   *Ask the Experts*

In conversation with Jerry Wilson:

Steps: *"From your own perspective of having achieved great success, what advice could you offer someone who's decided to start up a business?"*

Wilson: *"I would first tell that person to ask a lot of questions, to turn every rock over and ask for help."*

Steps: *"To whom?"*

Wilson: *"To people who have successfully travelled a similar road."*

In a culture where knowledge is regarded as a form of power, many people are afraid of that simple little statement, "I don't know." They are not only afraid of saying it, but even of thinking it. Understandable though it may be, this attitude is especially dangerous for a new businessperson. It is one thing to believe in yourself, but quite another to believe you have expertise that you actually don't. As an Oriental proverb puts it, "You can't learn anything unless you know you're a student."

Let's say you've started a graphic design and printing service. You know you've got a great eye for design, and you've done some pretty impressive work with computers. Does that make you an expert in the computer graphics business? Of course not. You may lack experience in adapting your creations to clients' needs, for instance. You may be unaware of some of the legal aspects of your business. You may not know where to get the best equipment deals. You may not know about which advertising venues are most and least productive. You may not know about electronic networks, newsletters or associations that could be useful to you. And so on.

When you're starting out, take stock of what you do and don't know. It might help to make a list. Jerry Wilson suggests getting in touch with ten people who have been highly successful in your chosen field of business. Take them out for lunch, with the intent of getting to know them and establishing connections. Offer to help them if appropriate, and go have a look at their working premises. And don't be afraid to ask questions from your "don't know" list. Remember that they too began from a position of not knowing.

Step 5 Get a Mentor

In conversation with Arthur Fettig:

Steps: *"I know you were in the safety equipment business and eventually moved on to the lecture circuit. How did you get from A to B?"*

Fettig: *"I heard a professional speaker—a man named Dr. G. Herbert True, from Notre Dame University—who knocked my eyes off when I saw him. I approached him, and eventually became his researcher. Then one day he hired me as his writer for the World Meeting Planners' Convention..."*

The mentor-apprentice relationship, which used to be the framework in which novices learned their trades or professions, is a dying institution. Perhaps the hectic pace of modern society has something to do with it; perhaps, too, since career changes have become the norm, beginners in a field are not necessarily young anymore and are therefore embarrassed to admit they're beginners. Whatever the reason, reluctance to seek a mentor can retard the process of acquiring expertise in a field.

What kind of people make good mentors? Generally speaking, they are people who have established such a high level of success in their fields that they do not feel threatened by newcomers nipping at their heels; people who have reached a phase in their careers where the natural next step is to share the information and experiences they've acquired over the years.

Fortunately for him, Arthur Fettig had no hesitations about seeking out a mentor. Prior to attending the lecture he refers to in the interview segment, Arthur had been writing humour articles for a few years. After the lecture, he saw his chance, and approached Dr. True with some suggestions for jokes that he might use in his speech. Herbert True was receptive, and soon became Arthur's mentor.

In a mentor-apprentice relationship, the day eventually comes when the apprentice breaks out on his or her own. For Arthur, that day came when he wrote the Meeting Planners' Convention speech for Dr. True. The audience was so moved that they didn't react for several minutes after Dr. True had finished, after which they rose to their feet in one motion and gave him a thunderous ovation. This told Arthur that he was ready to tackle the speaking circuit on his own, which he did shortly thereafter. He has never looked back.

Step 6: Observe Your Role Models

In conversation with Arthur Fettig:

Steps: *"You've written a book about how to captivate an audience. What I'm wondering is, is it more a matter of technique or of charisma?"*

Fettig: *"Both, of course. The interesting thing is that when I asked top-flight speakers what their techniques were, none of them could tell me—they really didn't know."*

Steps: *"So how did you figure it out?"*

Fettig: *"By observation. By watching hundreds of speakers, I started to see a pattern. This pattern is the basis of my book."*

Innovation is always based on observation. All "new" creations, such as books, musical compositions, or entrepreneurial ideas, are brought into being through a process of observing and building on what already exists. One way of "observing" successful people is by reading a book such as this one, which delivers first-hand insights into what makes these people tick. But there is no substitute for seeing and hearing for yourself.

Rather than accept that public speaking was a mysterious and unexplainable art, as the speakers he interviewed would have him believe, Art Fettig decided to watch them and decide for himself. It wasn't simply a question of watching, though. He analyzed their behaviour, and found that most good speakers started by conveying a larger-than-life image for a minute or two, then quickly cutting themselves down to size. "First there's this giant image, then they convey the feeling that they're just regular guys, like you and me," Art explains. "That combination is powerful." Another thing he found was that effective speakers always grabbed the audience right off the bat, rather than warm up slowly.

Art gained further insights into the body of a speech, which he calls the Message, and the winding-down process at the end. It didn't take him long to apply and refine these techniques in his own speeches.

Step 7 — Work Backwards From Your Goals

In conversation with Marilyn Jennings:

Steps: *"What is the best way to achieve a goal?"*

Jennings: *"Instead of setting yourself the vague goal of working hard and getting as much business as you can, start from the bottom line you desire and work backwards from there."*

Working backwards means thinking in terms of results and actions—in other words, "In order to get A, I have to do B. In order to get B, I have to do C. In order to do C ..."

When Marilyn Jennings arrived in Calgary, she decided that she'd had enough of being average and was ready for big-time success. Her reasoning went as follows: she wanted to earn a membership in the million dollar club. In order to do that, she would have to earn at least $100,000 within the year. In order to do that, she would have to bring in about $9,000 per month. In order to do that, she would have to sell three properties at an average commission of $3,000 every month. In order to do that, she would have to list about fifteen properties per month. (A typical ratio of sales to listings is about one to five, according to Marilyn.) In order to do that, she contacted at least fifty prospective vendors every day, using techniques described elsewhere in this book.

This is what Marilyn means by working backwards, and it certainly worked for her. By the end of the year, she had earned $130,000—well above her target.

 # Take the Time to Find Out What Your Client Wants

In conversation with Marilyn Jennings:

Steps: *"It seems that you qualify every client by way of an interview before you go out and see them."*

Jennings: *"Yes, I would never show anyone a home unless they first talked to me. In Calgary, when people would call me up wanting to see a house, I'd ask them to come in for an interview, and it always worked out that there were 20 to 30 people who said no, I want to see the house right now. So I'd turn those people over to another realtor."*

It is tempting to rush in on a potential sale—for example, to hurry off to meet a home buyer who calls you on the phone and asks to see one of your properties immediately.

Marilyn Jennings became convinced that this was not a productive way to sell properties after she started keeping a log of her business activities. She found that she was least likely to close a sale with clients whom she hadn't interviewed in advance. Also, since she didn't have much specific information about those clients' needs, she would end up showing them dozens of properties that turned out to be inappropriate. Having come to these conclusions, Marilyn made it a policy never to take on a client without a preliminary interview.

Marilyn's insights can be applied to any type of business. The more information you gain about your client's needs, the more you can target your product or service to those needs, the less time you need spend on inappropriate sales efforts, and the more likely you will close the sale. Less time, more sales.

Step 9: Be Loyal to Your Expertise

Steps: *"I've heard so much about you. What interests me is your concept of 'packaging an individual.' "*

Grosman: *"What I am talking about is the demise of linear employment—you know, the old nine-to-five-'til-sixty-five style. That's history. Whether self-employed or working for a large corporation, people have to think of themselves as contract employees."*

Steps: *"Even Mr. Joe Office Manager down at the local widget supplier?"*

Grosman: *"Yes, even him. He is a contract employee who moves from assignment to assignment within his company. So he has to package himself as a versatile and multi-skilled individual, just as an independent businessperson does."*

It is no longer useful for you to be loyal to a company, or even to a type of industry. Today's way of doing business dictates that your primary loyalty be to your own competence and expertise. In the first place, of course, you will have to acquire that expertise. Entrepreneurs in particular must be careful to develop a set of skills that can be transferred from industry to industry. To survive in the globally competitive economy of the nineties and beyond, you will have to be highly versatile. You will need to promote your product or service to a number of very different employers. What you are selling, in essence, is yourself.

This is not to say that you should package yourself as a Jack-of-all-trades, a generalist without a particular focus. On the contrary, it is usually to your advantage to present yourself as a specialist within each sector of your market. As long as you are satisfying your clients, they need not know that you are "specializing" in more than one area.

For example, if you're operating a paralegal service, your firm might be handling employment, family, and healthcare issues. Depending on your client, you can position yourself as a specialist in one or another of these areas. This is not misleading or dishonest if you have actually acquired the skills associated with each specialty.

And that, says Brian Grosman, is what it comes down to: acquiring the skills that enable you to package—and repackage— yourself in response to each new situation.

 *Start With the People Who Know You*

In conversation with Patricia Fripp:

Steps: *"What advice would you give to someone who is just starting out in the speaking business? Say it's a real estate agent, and he wants to do speaking engagements and gradually build himself up."*

Fripp: *"Very easy. You start with everybody on your Christmas-card list and you put together a speech."*

It is often said that charity starts at home. The same can be said about business, especially a new business venture.

If you're just starting out, you may not know people in your new field, but you certainly know people. Rather than trying to persuade strangers to do business with you, it makes sense to focus on the people who already know you and trust you.

To use Patricia Fripp's example, starting with the people on your Christmas-card list is a good idea if you make sure your speech is of interest to a diverse group of people. If you're a realtor, you could give a speech about the five things people need to know before buying a house. But you need not restrict yourself to your current area of expertise. You could choose something funny, or even talk about the process of writing and giving speeches.

After you've prepared your speech, Patricia suggests telling everybody on your Christmas-card list that you have a half-hour speech on such-and-such topic and would like an invitation to whatever club they may belong to, such as a rotary club or parents' association. Chances are you'll get more than one invitation. And since you will be speaking to people you already know, it will be relatively easy to ask them for written testimonials after you've given the speech.

This process—starting with the people you know, and using them as referrals for future business—can be applied to just about any type of business.

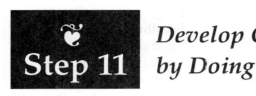

Step 11: Develop Confidence by Doing

In conversation with Peter Oliver:

Steps: *"You're considered among businesspeople to be very successful. Tell me a little bit about how you got to be where you are."*

Oliver: *"One thing I've found in the restaurant business is that if one is perceived as trying too hard, this can come across as insecurity and a lack of confidence. Being the best at what you do leads to a certain inner confidence that customers, staff and employees can feel."*

Steps: *"Right. And how do you build confidence?"*

Oliver: *"Confidence comes after accomplishment, not before it. The only way to build confidence is by doing."*

We're all good at reading up on what we have to do, at making lists of what we have to do, but we tend to be a little less disciplined when it comes to actually doing those things. For Peter Oliver, this ability to do—as opposed to think or talk about doing—is what sets apart the big-league players.

The techniques he suggests are simple enough: taking time every morning to prepare for the tasks of the day; keeping a notebook at all times so you can jot down ideas when they occur to you; and scheduling unpleasant tasks at the beginning rather than the end of the day, when they tend to be "forgotten."

Peter is extensively involved in fundraising, and one of the things he is less than enthusiastic about doing is calling people up to ask them for financial support. But he knows that there is no substitute for making those calls. The more he phones and asks people, the more people say no and the more people say yes. So on those days when fundraising calls are on his to-do list, he forces himself to make these calls first thing in the morning, whether he's in the mood or not—an attitude that can be thought of as "reverse procrastination."

Step 12: Give a Performance That Exceeds Your Fee

In conversation with Patricia Fripp:

Steps: *"What separates you from everybody else? There are so many people who want to speak in various parts of the continent. There must be something you are doing that makes you different from all the others."*

Fripp: *"When it comes to performance, I think it's very important to give a performance that exceeds your fee. Especially during a recession, people are going to question whether they're really getting value for what the speaker is charging."*

One of the temptations of doing business with many different clients is to expend our energy in proportion to our fee. If we feel we're underpaid, we underproduce. This attitude leads to a vicious cycle of mediocre work for mediocre pay. The only way out of the cycle is to work at 100% of our capacity without regard for how much we're getting paid. What eventually happens is that the high quality of our work is noticed, our reputation is strengthened, word spreads, and in time we attract clients who are able to pay us a higher fee.

It was this philosophy that enabled Patricia Fripp to gradually raise her speaking fee from zero to $3,500 in less than ten years. Because she gives her all to each performance—"melts things to death," as she puts it—she has no trouble attracting clients at that fee, even in times of financial restraint.

Patricia believes that people have less patience than they used to, and demand both substance and showmanship from public speakers. She pays attention to those little extras, such as handouts containing the key points of her presentation. She does not speak in the dark, even when using slides or overhead projectors, because "the speaker, not the overhead, is the star of the show." Above all, she makes sure that her speeches contain practical advice that people can take home with them and use the next day.

Step 13: Don't Brood Over Your Mistakes—Just Fix Them

In conversation with Peter Oliver:

Steps: *"You seem so positive and successful. Do you ever get down? How do you deal with snags or mistakes?"*

Oliver: *"Anyone who's involved in business will have their fair share of disappointments, but I tend to see them as a reflection of myself and I never hold someone else responsible for one of my failures. And then I say I'll fix it, and just keep banging away until I make it work."*

Steps: *"Give me an example of a business problem that you've learned to deal with."*

Oliver: *"Well, one thing that comes to mind is a star employee who quits. I used to think it would be impossible to replace someone that good, and get down about that. Now my attitude is that no matter who we have to replace, I will always make sure the replacement is even better. And it works."*

There's the ideal world, where once you get a contract, all you have to do is deliver the product or service required and then you get paid. And then there's the real world, where production snags, late payments, defects and other errors, cloud and complicate the picture.

Sooner or later, smart entrepreneurs come to realize that the glitches that intrude on perfection are simply part of the process, and learn to take them in stride. This is not to say that you shouldn't try to keep these glitches to an absolute minimum. However, rather than seeing them as "exceptions," it is more productive to treat them as problems to be solved, and to remember that no matter how irate a client may seem, good will is likely to be restored if you rectify the problem with promptness and professionalism.

The worst thing you can do is to regard the problem as a piece of bad luck that "surely won't strike again the next time." This prevents you from an honest examination of the conditions that gave rise to the problem. As Peter Oliver notes, taking responsibility for your business problems is the first step toward their resolution.

Step 14 — Don't Confuse Sensation With Success

In conversation with Jerry Goodis:

Steps: *"This book is about success, and you're certainly a shining example of it. If you don't mind, though, I'd like to hear about some of your failures."*

Goodis: *"I enjoy talking about my failures, because I and my staff have gotten our best laughs from them, and besides, they've all been learning experiences."*

Steps: *"Any examples that come to mind?"*

Goodis: *"Oh yes, there was the incident with Ovaltine... It looked like a sensational ad campaign on the surface, but the bottom line was, we didn't increase our customer's sales."*

Success in business is ultimately measured by the ability to generate revenues—by that and nothing else. Everything else you do is just preparation for that final event of exchanging goods or services for money.

It is easy to lose sight of this basic fact when trying to gauge the effectiveness of a business idea. Say you've just opened a colour film and printing operation, and you decide that you need some exceptional brochures to spread the word about your service. You have the brochures designed and printed, complete with raised lettering and gold-leaf appliques, and get showered with compliments from everyone who sees it. All this fuss can give you the illusion of success, even if (for one reason or another) the brochure isn't helping you generate more sales.

The incident Jerry Goodis refers to occurred in the mid-sixties, when Ovaltine approached his agency in concern over their declining sales. The problem was that old people were the primary consumers of their product—a powder you're supposed to mix with milk and drink at bedtime—while young people were busy drinking trendier products like Coke and Pepsi. So Jerry and his staff devised a campaign aimed at the youth market. "You can get to sleep with me tonight," was the clever, double-edged slogan. The campaign was a sensational success in terms of getting attention for Ovaltine. The company received hundreds of enthusiastic letters from young people who had seen the ad. They didn't buy the product—they were still drinking Coke and Pepsi—but they thought the ad was terrific. The company also got irate letters from their actual consumers, who accused them of being in poor taste and stopped buying the product. The result was that Ovaltine nearly went out of business.

The lesson of that story, says Jerry, is that you have to be honest in evaluating whether your successes are really $ucce$$e$.

Step 15 Give an Inch, Get a Mile

In conversation with Alex Tilley:

Steps: *"Your customer service is outstanding by any standards. Why do you always push yourself to provide that little bit more than everybody else?"*

Tilley: *"Two reasons. One, I honestly care about my customers. I want them to be happy when they open a package from Tilley's. And the other, more self-serving reason, is that I want to keep those customers for life."*

When he has a clothing shipment delivered to a customer, Alex Tilley often includes a little gift, such as the recently published book on travel tips written by his daughter Allison and illustrated by cartoonist Ben Wicks. The gift is always hand-wrapped, with a personal thank-you note attached.

While giving away a book may seem like a large investment in proportion to the value of a few items of clothing, Alex takes the long-range view—he wants to keep his customers for life. And it is often those small, unexpected gestures that stand out most strongly in customers' minds and secure their long-term loyalty.

An example of this principle in Alex's own life is that he once selected a man as his realtor for the single reason that, following a previous business transaction, the man had sent him some particularly stunning poinsettias. "That little thing got him my business," recalls Alex. "It was a $15 investment, and it paid off in spades."

The little extras you provide need not exceed your means. If you are a small and fairly informal business, such as a desktop publishing service, you might send—about a month ahead of Christmas—five handpainted or potato-print cards to your steady clients, which they in turn can use as Christmas cards. The gesture is whimsical, original, and sure to get you noticed among the crowd of card senders.

It's the spirit that counts, and if the spirit you convey is "I value your business," then your gesture has been successful.

Step 16   *Learn to Take Rejection in Stride*

In conversation with Hugh Rennie:

Steps: *"Everybody is talking about 'positive thinking' these days. How do you see the role of positive thinking in entrepreneurial success?"*

Rennie: *"The quality you're talking about comes especially handy when you've suffered some kind of rejection."*

Steps: *"Is it a quality you can develop, or do you have to be born with it?"*

Rennie: *"You can definitely develop it. But first, you have to come to grips with yourself as a person. You have to learn to like yourself and believe in yourself no matter what happens to you. And this takes mental discipline."*

There are two basic reasons for rejection. One is that your work is substandard, and the other is that the client doesn't need your services at the time. Unless you have actual proof that you've been turned down because your product or service is not good enough, you should assume that the rejection is not personal.

A common trap people fall into is the "always" or "never" thinking pattern, as in "I'll *never* be able to accomplish this," or "This always happens to me." Remind yourself that two or three negative experiences don't add up to a "never." This is easier to see if you're dealing with a less charged situation, such as leaving your keys inside your locked car. If this happens to you once or twice, does it follow that it always happens? Of course not. The same applies to any rejections you may encounter in business.

Hugh says, "A person who gets into a state of despair has to learn to redirect their way of thinking. If you're tempted to think that you're a loser, or that a situation is hopeless, stop and realign yourself. Remind yourself of your strengths, your past successes. Look at yourself in the mirror and say, 'Damn, I'm good.'"

Hugh acknowledges that it's not enough to tell yourself these things; you have to support them with actions like continually upgrading your skills, and readjusting any behaviours that may have gotten in your way. In other words, in order to combat feelings of rejection on a deeper level, you need be both positive and honest with yourself.

Section 2

Marketing

The Method Behind the Mystery

Step 1 — Market a Need, Not a Service

In conversation with Jo Stumpf:

Steps: *"You must have had some sort of method or system to get where you were going."*

Stumpf: *"Marketing. Marketing communicates what you have to offer to your customer that compels them to desire you over your competitors—and for their self-serving reasons, not yours."*

Steps: *"In other words, put the interest of the customer ahead of your own interest."*

Stumpf: *"Right. I don't susbscribe to personal marketing. Don't tell people that you are a superstar; they don't care. What they care about are their needs."*

It is tempting to pump up our achievements when making a sales pitch. We make the error of assuming that blue-chip client lists and professional awards will persuade a potential client to do business with us. While it may be advantageous to discreetly communicate a few of our more impressive achievements, this approach should not form the basis of a marketing plan.

The first thing to do is to put yourself in your client's shoes. What does the client stand to gain from your product or service? In practical terms, will the client save money, gain customers, or free up badly needed time, by doing business with you? If you believe that the answer is yes, then it is up to you to back up your conviction with facts and guarantees.

Jo Stumpf determined that his clients had one need: they wanted to know that when they signed a listing grant, they weren't stuck in it and could get out of it at any time. He then positioned himself as posing less of a risk than other realtors, and backed up his claim with guarantees such as taking $500 off his commission if he didn't sell the property within 90 days, or taking $100 off his commission if he didn't return calls within 24 hours. In other words, he put himself on the line—and saw a dramatic improvement in his bottom line.

Step 2 Market Steadily, Not In Spurts

In conversation with Patricia Fripp:

Steps: *"How does a business like yours survive a recession?"*

Fripp: *"First and foremost, by delivering quality at all times. And when it comes to promotion, I do it all the time, not in spurts."*

Steps: *"You mean you're always there, flogging your business to potential clients?"*

Fripp: *"Well, that's part of it, but it's also a question of becoming well known in your community. I believe you can be a hero in your hometown."*

Many people running their own business think of marketing as something you do if the need arises—that is, if your sales drop and you need to get more clients. This is a reactive approach, and leads to a rise-and-fall pattern of business activity. No matter how much work is coming in today, you need to devote regular time (meaning *every* week) to promoting your business. This is easy enough to understand in theory, but when things are going well and clients are pounding on your door, it is easy to lose sight of the need to market steadily.

Patricia Fripp divides her marketing efforts into shorter- and longer-term strategies. Her short-term strategies include providing her clients and audiences with personal items, such as calendars or day-planners, that have her name on them. She also advertises consistently in the Yellow Pages, and supplies her clients and potential clients with custom-tailored articles.

Longer-term marketing strategies are often ignored by entrepreneurs because the results of such strategies are neither immediate nor directly measurable. But Patricia believes they are the key to the longevity and success of her business. She gets interviewed and quoted in all the media, publishes regular newsletters, belongs to five convention and visitors' bureaus in the chamber of commerce, and does targeted showcases. And rather than regard other speakers as competition, she establishes partnerships with them, which in the long run benefits all parties.

Step 3: Market to Your Inactive Clients

In conversation with Jo Stumpf:

Steps: *"Marketing is such a general topic. How can I, as a businessperson, take advantage of what you are telling me about marketing?"*

Stumpf: *"First and foremost, you should be marketing to our inactive clients. Your greatest source of business is turning your client base into a sales force. You must go back and tell your clients on a consistent and constant basis—not once, not twice, but monthly—why it is to the advantage of their friends, family members, people they know at work or school, to do business with you. Always go back to your clients."*

Over the months and years, you should be expanding your list of inactive clients. These will include former clients, personal acquaintances you think would benefit from your business, people you met at professional functions, people whose names were given to you by business associates, and people in the same professions as your current clients, to name a few.

On a regular basis—perhaps at the beginning of each new month—you should block off a period of time in which you call each and every person on your inactive client list. In some cases the call will be brief and low-key, and in others the time will be ripe for a more direct approach. It's up to you to assess the urgency of the person's need and how responsive they are likely to be to your pitch.

The key in making these follow-up calls, as in everything else. is consistency.

As Jo Stumpf advises, you should be turning your inactive clients into a sales force—in other words, using them as a source of referrals. To sweeten the pie for them, you can offer incentives (such as future discounts) to those clients whose referrals end up in new business for you. You can also provide *them* with referrals, and you should certainly take advantage of every opportunity you have to pass along information that may be of use to them, such as newspaper clippings pertinent to their business, lectures that may interest them, discounts on equipment, etc. The idea is to be an unobtrusive but steady presence in their minds.

Step 4   Market to Your Active Clients

In conversation with Jerry Wilson:

Wilson: *"The biggest mistake people make in business is that after the consummation of a sale, they put the client on the back burner."*

Steps: *"What should they be doing instead?"*

Wilson: *"As far as I'm concerned, a sale is the beginning, not the end, of a relationship. It's the point at which your marketing blitz should kick in."*

Almost all successful businesspeople will tell you that repeat business is a large part of their revenue. In order to build a thriving repeat clientele, you have to do at least three things: (1) provide superior quality in your product or service; (2) charge reasonable prices, and (3) market to your active clients—that is, those past and present clients who still have a need for your business.

Let them know about product enhancements, add-ons, and price savings for repeat purchases. Most importantly, according to Jerry Wilson, you should follow up on how they are doing as a result of doing business with you in the past. For instance, if you've redesigned an office interior, find out if there are any problems with traffic flow, or if some areas are not getting enough light. If the answer is yes, perhaps you can suggest further changes or equipment upgrades. Show an interest in how your business has affected their own day-do-day operations.

In Jerry Wilson's business, repeat contracts are not very common. When people hire him as a professional speaker, they usually think it's a one-shot deal. But Jerry estimates that 80% of his clients end up doing business with him again, a figure he attributes to his policy of marketing to his active clients. "There is a great benefit to doing business with repeat clients," he says, "because the second time around, you know the client extremely well, and you can probably do a much better job for them at less cost."

Step 5: Make Supporters Out of Non-Clients

In conversation with Harry Rosen:

Steps: *"From your first location on Parliament Street until you expanded, you wanted a certain kind of market. What did you have to do in order to get this specific market?"*

Rosen: *"The approach we took in our little store on Parliament Street was that whether an individual who walked in was a prospective buyer or not, they shouldn't be ignored. Perhaps they couldn't afford what we were doing, but they might carry the message to someone else who could."*

Steps: *"Do you have proof that this actually happened?"*

Rosen: *"Yes, lots of times. You'd be surprised how often we were promoted by someone who brought in the express parcels and had a brother-in-law who later turned up at our store to buy something."*

While it makes sense to direct your marketing efforts to those people who have the potential to become your customers, this doesn't mean that people who don't fall into this group should be ignored if they cross your path. In fact, Harry Rosen found these non-customers to be a steady source of future business. It's not that he marketed directly to these people, but if they happened to walk into his store for whatever reason, or if he came across them throughout the course of his day, he befriended them and communicated his vision to them. He found that when people believed in his sincerity and admired what he was doing, they would support him in their own way, usually by "recommending us to others even though they weren't consumers themselves."

In the early days especially, Harry's intent was to turn people into either customers or "carriers of the message." In order to create such carriers, of course, Harry and his staff had to communicate the uniqueness of his enterprise to everyone they spoke with. "If you're thought of as unique," he says now, "people simply want to talk about you. They end up doing your marketing for you. And if you can find the key to activating that mechanism, you have found the essence of success."

Step 6: Stay Away From Institutional Advertising

In conversation with Jo Stumpf:

Stumpf: *"Most advertisements have the company logo on top and that's meaningless."*

Steps: *"Can you expand a bit on this last point?"*

Stumpf: *"Eliminate institutional advertising. It is a waste of money. Write a very compelling headline instead."*

What draws people's attention to a printed ad? Certainly not tired old copy like "Just sold" or "We're number one." Although it is practically guaranteed that readers' eyes will sail right past this type of copy, many advertisers continue to churn out these generic headlines.

Such headlines, says Jo Stumpf, have as much impact as floral wallpaper. No matter how compelling the inside copy is, if the headline doesn't do its job, the inside copy will never get read.

To be effective, a headline should sound fresh and catchy. Humour is always a good device, since it helps people drop their guard, which makes them more receptive to the content of the ad. For instance, instead of the clichéd "Just sold" on your drop-off flyer, Jo suggests something like, "You heard what your neighbour did last night, didn't you?" The reader's curiosity will be piqued, and it's a good bet that he or she will get to the fine print.

 # Don't Spend Indiscriminately On Marketing

In conversation with Jerry Goodis:

Steps: *"How would you define marketing, as opposed to selling?"*

Goodis: *"I have to admit that I'm sometimes annoyed by all this semantic quibbling. Marketing gets all kind of fancy definitions these days. People assume it is a mysterious science and that if you spend megabucks, you'll get results, as if by magic."*

Steps: *"So the results are not in proportion to the money spent?"*

Goodis: *"No. Results are more a function of the suitability of a marketing campaign than on its budget."*

Jerry Goodis's experience is that when it comes to marketing or advertising, more isn't necessarily better. Television ads are not necessarily more effective than print ads, though they may be more glamorous to work on. Jerry finds it deplorable that many agencies recommend TV advertising to their clients as a matter of course. What they should be doing instead, he says, is some thorough and honest research on how to best to reach the client's target market. This will not necessarily be through television advertising, even if the client has the budget for it.

Similarly, when promoting yourself to clients, you shouldn't assume that you need to spend lots of money to have an impact. In fact, Jerry advises going as cheaply as you can without sacrificing the essence of your message. For example, one of his entrepreneurship students, a Chinese Canadian woman of 28, was in a position to show CEOs how to save considerable amounts of money on their personal tax returns, but she had trouble getting clients on the phone. She also didn't have a lot of money to spend on marketing. Jerry told her to go down to Chinatown and buy 25 abacuses ("The Chinese invented the abacus, so she might as well capitalize on her heritage."), send them to 25 of her prime targets, along with a note saying, "You can use an abacus to figure out your taxes, or you can use me. I have a completely legal way of saving you important tax money, and if you'll give me 15 minutes of your time, I'll show you how."

The woman called him six weeks later with the news that she had obtained work from McDonald's and several other major corporations, all from an investment of about $250.

Step 8   Educate, Don't Sell

In conversation with Jo Stumpf:

Stumpf: *"Another important principle in creating ads is to educate readers rather than sell to them."*

Steps: *"Does that mean you don't promote your product or service?"*

Stumpf: *"Not necessarily. But the meat of your ad should be education, followed up by an offer of some kind."*

The ceaseless stream of advertising in the printed and broadcast media is producing an increasingly sophisticated population of consumers. Getting people to do business with you is no longer a matter of simply telling them what a wonderful person or organization you are.

For example, if you're trying to appeal to first-time home buyers, why not send them an information package which contains a chart comparing total monthly payments (under various mortgage plans) to paying rent? This is what Jo Stumpf calls educating the reader. To complete the package, he suggests including an offer of a free video, magazine or first homebuyer's guide. And be sure to tell readers what's in it for them if they order the publication—for instance, that it provides answers to "the seven most important questions to ask your lender before you sign anything."

Once a reader orders the material (which comes with more information about your product or service), he or she is much farther along the road to becoming your client.

 # Step 9 — Send a Consistent Message to Consumers

In conversation with Harry Rosen:

Steps: *"How do you market yourself? Is it primarily by means of advertising?"*

Rosen: *"Of course we do advertising, but our most effective marketing happens right in the store. Our store has to be a magnet, it has to be a theatre, it has to be exciting, it has to pull the customer in."*

Steps: *"You're talking about the actual stores as a marketing device, a means of attracting people?"*

Rosen: *"Sure. This is our way of advertising our history and product. And everything has to be consistent—the window displays, the interior displays, the people in our store. Our staff should personify our ideas."*

If your marketing is inconsistent, you will do nothing but confuse the consumer. For instance, if you've positioned yourself as a supplier of a high-end product for an exclusive group of buyers, and your sales staff emphasizes price wars, then you're confusing the consumer. If you have marketed yourself as a service-oriented operation, and your staff looks bored or is unavailable on the floor, then you are confusing the consumer. If your marketing angle is beat-the-competition pricing, and your actual pricing is the same as everywhere else, then you are confusing the consumer.

Speaking about his own business, Harry Rosen says, "You have to understand how consumers think, and you have to give them simple messages which you communicate via your store's appearance." One of the things he tries to communicate is low-key, home-style warmth. When people approach a Harry Rosen store, he makes sure there is nothing threatening or intimidating to draw them away. And when they walk in, the staff makes them feel "as welcome as if they were walking into someone's home."

Harry recalls a friend telling him years ago that "There is nothing worse than setting expectations you can't deliver." In other words, think long and hard before making a business promise. You will be judged much more critically if you make a promise you can't keep than if you don't make any promise at all. Delivering on claims is "a never-ending task," according to Harry, but the payoff is a business that keeps on thriving.

 # Use Testimonials in Your Advertising

In conversation with Alex Tilley:

Steps: *"Has your television advertising been effective?"*

Tilley: *"We think so, we're not sure. Also, I'm a great believer in testimonials far more than anything else."*

Steps: *"So the bottom line is that what people say about you is important?"*

Tilley: *"Damn right it's important—testimonials are my credentials."*

A good word from a customer can go a long way. Nobody knows this more than Alex Tilley, whose experience has led him to believe that testimonials are among the most effective marketing devices. That is why he encourages his customers to call or write with feedback, and displays their written testimonials in his stores.

Alex believes that every businessperson, regardless of their field, can use testimonials to their advantage. "If I were a realtor," he speculates, "I would keep a whole list of nice comments people have said about me. I wouldn't go out there empty-handed—I would tell prospective clients, 'Here are the names and addresses of 20 people who have dealt with me.'"

Alex's television advertising program is built around testimonials. It is very cost-effective, he says, because he can get several short testimonial ads into a 24-hour period. He also sprinkles his catalogues (with customers' permission, of course) with testimonials, including those of a former premier, a former governor general, and the wife of Charlton Heston.

As Alex candidly admits, what people think of you is important to your business, and can serve as a powerful marketing tool.

 # Step 11 — Market By Varied and Repeated Exposure

In conversation with Jerry Wilson:

Steps: *"You seem to be tireless in your marketing and advertising efforts."*

Wilson: *"The challenge is to keep that 'window of awareness' open in people's minds."*

Steps: *"What you seem to be saying is that it's important for your name to keep popping up everywhere."*

Wilson: *"Yes, but you cannot just do it randomly. You have to do it methodically and intentionally."*

Studies have shown that it takes three to six exposures before an ad makes an impression. For this reason, it is not productive to run an ad once, then yank it out immediately if it doesn't produce the results you hoped for.

Say you've decided to advertise your "How to get your book published" workshop in the Saturday classified-ad section of a major newspaper, and after the first ad you get only a sprinkling of calls. This does not necessarily mean you should stop running the ad in that spot. If you've done your homework and determined that the newspaper has the right readership and a good track-record with classified advertisers, you should run your ad for at least three consecutive Saturdays before making any decisions. This is what Jerry Wilson means by a "methodical and intentional" approach.

On the other hand, you need not restrict yourself to one venue when marketing your product or service. Jerry believes that in this over-stimulated society, it's important to make what he calls "multiple impressions." When he organized a major trade show, for instance, he didn't limit himself to television or newspaper ads. He produced video and print materials previewing the event, sent humorous faxes about the upcoming show to former clients, and instructed his contacts to spread the word in various ways. His goal was to make his trade show the talk of the town. In fact, during the event itself, someone came up to him and said, "What in the world are you doing? I must have heard about this show at least 20 times." To which Jerry replied, "Well, you're here, aren't you?"

Step 12 — Use Silliness As a Marketing Strategy

In conversation with Jerry Goodis:

Steps: *"You seem to have a bottomless bag of marketing tricks."*

Goodis: *"Yes, and they get cornier and cornier. And at the risk of sounding a little boastful, some of them are quite innovative."*

Steps: *"You used the word 'corny.' Can you tell us about a corny marketing ploy that has worked for you?"*

Goodis: *"Every time I sent a CEO a cherry pie with a note saying, 'I know you want a bigger slice of the market'—I mean, what could be cornier than that—I got a call back, and I often ended up getting a contract."*

If you think other people would be annoyed or offended at your "silly" marketing idea, ask yourself what your own reaction would be if you were on the receiving end. Jerry Goodis believes that people aren't getting enough silliness in their lives and crave more of it. "We're all little children at heart," he says, "with bodies that look grown up. We love getting presents and toys, especially if they make a statement about the issue at hand."

One of Jerry's favorite silly ideas is his "apples-and-orange" scheme. Here's how it goes: Identify 25 prospects for the product or service you're selling. Then send each of these 25 prospects a fresh apple (in a square silver box wrapped up with a bow) along with the message, "Comparing my ___ to the others is like comparing apples and..." Leave the sentence unfinished, and the next day, send those same people an orange, packaged the same way, with the end of the sentence, "...and oranges." When you follow up with phonecalls, you can give more information about your product or service.

Another idea, which he suggested to an engineer who believed he could save clients money by designing or redesigning their facilities, was to get an old cash register—the bulky, 75-pound variety that nobody uses anymore—and mail it (sequentially) to his best prospects, along with a written message about how he could make their cash register ring by designing their facilities more intelligently than anybody else in the country.

The response? The architectural firms who received his cash register all told him it was the dumbest thing they'd ever heard of, and they all made appointments to see him and discuss his design ideas. Jerry doesn't know the final outcome, but the man certainly got a hearing, which wouldn't have happened if he had sent the usual letters, flyers or brochures.

Section 3

Organization
The Well-Oiled Machine

Step 1  Schedule Meetings With Yourself

In conversation with Harold Taylor:

Steps: *"The word 'prioritizing' gets a lot of air time these days. In a practical sense, what does it mean?"*

Taylor: *"It means figuring out what the important things are in advance, and then blocking off, say, an hour and a half next Thursday to do these things. You have your calls intercepted by voice mail, and don't let visitors into your working space. You are incognito for that time."*

Steps: *"It seems so simple, when you put it that way."*

Taylor: *"Simple, but people say they don't have time to sequester themselves for an hour an a half. So I ask them, 'How do you have time to talk to me right now?' And they say, 'Well, I guess it's because I've scheduled this time to talk to you.'"*

Certain tasks, such as writing a proposal, preparing a budget or marketing plan, or revamping the company brochure, require steady concentration and can only be accomplished effectively in the absence of interruptions. Many people have trouble sticking to their resolve to accomplish such tasks at a specific time. The problem, according to Harold Taylor, is that people believe that the interruptions—potential customers, clients, people with questions— are crises that have to be dealt with right away. In truth, there are very few crises that won't wait for the hour or two it takes you to finish that task.

If you've identified something as a priority, presumably it's because it *has* to get done as soon as possible; not doing it will have an adverse effect on sales or client relations, or interfere with a goal you've set for your business. So then it's a question of scheduling a meeting with yourself, as though you were one of your own clients, and sticking to the "agenda" for that meeting.

Step 2 — Don't Be a Packrat

In conversation with Harold Taylor:

Steps: *"Can you talk some more about being organized?"*

Taylor: *"First of all, I'd like to say that I wasn't always so organized. In fact, through lack of time management, I found myself in some pretty hot water and my business almost went bankrupt. It took me about eight years to truly get organized."*

Steps: *"Can you give us a simple example of good organizational skills?"*

Taylor: *"Yes. A basic tenet is not hanging on to every piece of paper that passes your desk."*

Concerning the dilemma of saving versus scrapping, the prevailing wisdom seems to be, "When in doubt, file." Harold Taylor believes that it is just as important to keep filing to a minimum as it is to keep every document, and he has arrived at a compromise which might be stated as, "When in doubt, file temporarily."

Say you've filed away the minutes of last week's meeting. If you decide that in three months, the information in those minutes will no longer be relevant to your work, write a throw-out date of three months from today on the top page, and when the time comes, just do it. Chances are the building won't come crashing down around your feet.

Another technique Harold has found useful is to sort the incoming paper into three piles: routine, important, and urgent. He then sets about working on the urgent pile, followed by the important pile. If he never gets to the third pile, he simply throws it out. The benefits of this method are less time spent rifling through stacks of paper, less clutter, and less aggravation—all of which result in a clearer head for doing business.

 **Step 3** *Keep an Organized Desk*

In conversation with Harold Taylor:

Taylor: *"The one thing you have to do is keep an organized desk."*

Steps: *"Does organized mean neat?"*

Taylor: *"Organized means you know where everything is and can access it immediately, which is more important than how neat your piles are."*

Steps: *"Are there any items you find essential to keep on your desk?"*

Taylor: *"I consider a telephone log essential. You have to have one area where you do the phone calls, and that's where I have my telephone log."*

Some people are naturally neat, and can't function well unless their desk is tidy. In moderation, such neatness is an asset because an uncluttered environment promotes uncluttered thinking. But an extreme compulsion for neatness can interfere with efficiency, because it drives people to spend excessive time doing things like sharpening pencils or reprinting documents with invisible flaws in them.

The kind of organization Harold Taylor is referring to is different from simple neatness, which is more a reflection of personal style than of good working habits. Being organized means not having to waste time rifling through papers, and not forgetting what was said during an important meeting or phone call because you failed to keep a written record of it.

Harold finds his telephone log invaluable as a record of his telephone communications. He makes a note of every phone call that goes in and every phone call that goes out, and what follow-up action is required on his part, if any. After he has completed the action, he crosses off the entry. If something hasn't been looked at by the end of the day, he puts it in his day planner for the following day. So in effect, his telephone log functions as an expansion of the current day's agenda and a feeder for the next day's agenda.

Step 4: Understand the Terms of Your Contract

In conversation with Brian Grosman:

Steps: *"Have there been any recent changes in the legal aspects of self-employment?"*

Grosman: *"Today, it's more important than ever to have a solid contract, especially for a complex or long-term project."*

Steps: *"Is it because the laws have become more complicated?"*

Grosman: *"The main reason is that the person who is hiring you may be gone by the time you've finished the work. So if nothing is in writing, nobody knows where they stand."*

It is a cold fact of today's business world that verbal contracts do not provide adequate protection, if ever they did. As Brian Grosman points out, the average duration of people's employment is much shorter than it used to be. No matter how well-intentioned your client or how clear the terms of your agreement, if the essential points are not in writing, you can be in trouble if the person who contracted you is different from the person to whom you deliver the finished product. The only instance in which it might not be necessary to have a written contract is for a very short-term project that does not involve much financial risk on your part.

You shouldn't be concerned about frightening off your client by insisting on a written document. Professionalism is always respected. Besides, a good contract offers protection to both parties, and minimizes the risk of bad feelings on either side after the work has been completed. The contract need not be in "legalese." You can create a draft yourself, which you can then discuss with your client and modify if necessary.

If you are an independent real estate agent, for example, your contract should contain an accurate description of your commission structure including increments and bonuses. It should also specify who is responsible for obtaining clients, your compensation if you are required leave the firm, and whether you have the right to take your client base with you. Finally, it should state the liabilities on either side in case of a breach of contract.

Brian Grosman is constantly surprised by the number of cases in which an independent agent is terminated after years of service with one agency and fails to obtain adequate compensation. In some cases, it is because there wasn't a proper contract. Just as often, however, the agent had a suitable contract but failed to understand its terms.

Step 5: Break Your Clients Down Into Categories

In conversation with Marilyn Jennings:

Steps: *"You say that you get clients without having to advertise."*

Jennings: *"Yes. I've never put an ad in the paper in the city of Calgary."*

Steps: *"So the next question is, how do you get your clients?"*

Jennings: *"I've broken down prospective clients into four categories, and am diligent about tapping into each one."*

It is generally accepted that breaking difficult tasks down into manageable chunks makes it easier to tackle them. The same principle holds true for anything else, including your list of prospective clients Breaking down a general concept such as "prospective client" into specific groups of people helps you focus on strategies for communicating with each group.

Marilyn Jennings' four categories are: clients she's already dealt with, prospects referred to her by former clients, prospects referred to her by friends or acquaintances, and prospects referred to her by a fellow realtor. This systematic classification helps Marilyn focus on strategies for filling up each group. For instance, she can spend time compiling a list all those people among her current and former acquaintances who might be in a position to refer new business to her. She has found that people in positions of influence, such as doctors or lawyers, are particularly good sources.

In addition to these four basic categories, Marilyn taps into the hundred neighbours around every listing that she writes. She talks to them personally at their door, and turns them into her personal sales force.

Step 6 — Create and Use a Follow-Up Schedule

In conversation with Jerry Goodis:

Goodis: *"The secret is to stay in regular touch. Not sporadic, but regular."*

Steps: *"Do you have a special system to do this?"*

Goodis: *"It's quite simple—you have to call clients on a regular schedule, like a dentist's office does."*

It is obviously important to keep in touch with your clients, prospects, and other business associates. But there is a big difference between doing this haphazardly and systematically. If you don't have a system, you run the risk of contacting people too infrequently, which causes them to forget about you, or too frequently, which causes them to get annoyed with you.

Jerry Goodis finds it hard to understand why most professionals are so poorly organized when it comes to doing these follow-up calls, and cites his dentist's office as a counterexample. "Somehow, the dentist's assistant manages to call me every three months, like clockwork. I don't have to make appointments myself, the office does it for me. If a dental office can be that well organized, why can't other businesses get their act together? If they did, they would get a higher income, more satisfied customers, and increase the level of respect in the community for their profession."

A simple but rarely used solution is to make up a special follow-up sheet, with the people to contact listed in the left-hand column, followed by rows of boxes for writing the date and content of each call. To the right of the last-used box, you can pencil in what you think is the best date to make the next follow-up call. When it's that time of the week you've set aside for making such calls, all you have to do is scan the contact sheet to see who you should be calling that week. That way nobody gets left out, and nobody gets pestered.

 *Step 7* — *Train Your Staff to Answer Phones Properly*

In conversation with Nancy Friedman:

Steps: *"I called your office the other day and was amazed. I felt immediately welcome. What was it about your receptionist that made me feel so welcome?"*

Friedman: *"She didn't have a choice. It's a condition of employment and grounds for termination."*

Steps: *"I think oar office really needs some training as far as your services are concerned."*

Friedman: *"Employers don't hire bad people, they hire untrained people. I'm constantly amazed at the lack of training. In any country."*

Have you ever called up a commercial office and had the receptionist mumble the name of the company so indistinctly that you weren't sure you'd called the right place? Have you ever dealt with a customer service representative whose voice was sharp with annoyance? According to Nancy Friedman, the bad vibes created by a poor telephone manner may not register consciously with callers, but they always register at some level. Perhaps without even knowing why, many callers will be dissuaded from doing business with companies whose staff is not answering the telephone properly

When asked about the best way to answer the phone, Nancy states that while there is no one-size-fits-all formula, your response should always include three elements. The first is a buffer such as Good morning, Good afternoon, or Happy Tuesday. It makes the caller feel welcome. The second is the company name, pronounced clearly, and the third is your own name. It is not necessary to include "How can l help you?" in your initial greeting. Nancy cautions that anything you say after your name has the effect of erasing your name.

As for things *not* to say on the telephone, Nancy lists five: "I don't know," "We can't do that," "Hang on a second," starting a sentence with the word No, and telling people what they have to do. Nancy's staff is not permitted to say these things, ever. She considers "no" to be an especially rejecting term, and trains her staff to find alternate ways to phrase a negative response.

 # Step 8 — Keep Your Receptionist Informed

In conversation with Nancy Friedman:

Steps: *"How should a receptionist answer the phone?"*

Friedman: *"Receptionists should be trained to answer as many questions as possible. It's more efficient that way. But sometimes there are questions a receptionist is not equipped to answer."*

Steps: *"And then what?"*

Friedman: *"He or she should know who the call goes to. And the only way to make sure of this is to include the receptionist in what goes on in the office."*

The more calls your receptionist can handle without assistance, the more efficient your operation, since those calls don't have to be forwarded to staff people who may be absent or too busy to respond immediately. Nancy Friedman considers a receptionist to be a company's first sales person—she *never* uses the phrase, "just a receptionist"—and believes that all receptionists should receive up front training of some kind. This training can be more or less formal, depending on the size and complexity of your operation. If you are running a small operation, you can simply make a list of the ten most common questions callers ask, and then go through the appropriate responses with your receptionist.

But this isn't enough. If you want the receptionist to be of maximal value to you, he or she must have a finger on the pulse of your business. And the only way that will happen is through communication. As Nancy puts it, "Receptionists are not mind readers. If they are to know everything, they need to be told absolutely everything."

It may not always be possible for receptionists to be physically present at meetings. At the very least, however, they should be given written memos outlining what went on during those meetings. In an advertising agency, for instance, if the receptionist has been informed that a particular account has been transferred to Jim Brown, then he or she will know to direct callers to that person, and the organization as a whole will appear professional and well-run.

Step 9 — Avoid "Wh—" Telephone Questions

In conversation with Nancy Friedman:

Steps: *"It's common to ask callers, 'Who am I speaking to?' if they don't identify themselves."*

Friedman: *"That is absolutely incorrect. It's not wrong, actually, just ineffective."*

Steps: *"So how do you get them to give you their name?"*

Friedman: *You will want to use the 'and...' technique, because when you're trying to get information from someone, 'Wh—' questions are very threatening."*

What is your name? Where do you live? Who referred you to us? When can you come in for an appointment? Although there is nothing technically wrong with asking such questions, Nancy Friedman believes they are intimidating—exactly the opposite of what you want, which is to put callers at ease.

The alternative is to use what Nancy calls the dot-dot-dot style of conversation. For instance, if a caller hasn't given you his or her name, you can say something like, "This is Jane White, and I'm speaking to..." In other words, you let the other person complete the sentence. It is a painless way to ask questions without sounding like an interrogator. It encourages a reply without forcing it.

To use another example, let's say a caller is looking to buy a word-processing software package but hasn't given you specific information about what kind of program he or she has in mind. Using the dot-dot-dot approach, you can drat out the caller with an open-ended statement like, "You're looking for a program with..." If the caller still doesn't provide the information you need, you can complete the sentence with a tentative suggestion such as, "...with graphics capabilities, and perhaps the ability to interface with other programs...?" Here again, the idea is to elicit a reply without forcing it.

If used properly, this style of questioning should sound very natural. In fact, Nancy finds herself using it in her personal as well as business conversations.

Step 10: Make It Easy For People to Do Business With You

In conversation with Jerry Wilson:

Steps: *"In your book, you talk about installing a 'no-hassle' business program. Can you tell me a little more about that?"*

Wilson: *"Quoting from the book: 'The difference between operating a business and operating a business with no hassle... can be summed up in one word— attitude.'"*

Steps: *"What does 'attitude" mean to you?"*

Wilson: *"As it relates to the concept of no hassle, attitude can be summed up by the sentence, 'I am going to make it as easy as possible for you to do business with me.'"*

How easy is it for people to do business with you? Are there umpteen forms to fill out and dozens of bureaucratic steps to plow through in order to complete a transaction? If you are a retailer, for instance, do your cashiers have to spend ten minutes entering information into their computers every time a customer buys an item? If you're running an accounting business, do you require your clients to do most of the information-gathering, receipt-sorting, adding, multiplying, and other drudge work for you, or do you take much of the load off their shoulders?

"Most businesspeople make it difficult for you to do business with them," Jerry Wilson believes. "There are so many rules and regulations. Clients don't understand all the paperwork or the legalities, and there's a kind of nightmare in that. So they stay away."

The first step in creating a no-hassle system is to organize and streamline your paper trail. Is this or that form really necessary? Can it be simplified, or made more visually appealing? Can two forms be condensed into one? Can you simplify some of the language in documents dealing with legal matters? Can you design a simpler and better system for keeping track of unpaid invoices or inventory on loan?

Streamline wherever possible, keeping in mind that your clients, like just about all humans, would rather follow a simple procedure than a convoluted one.

Section 4

Creative Thinking

The Power of Ideas

Step 1 — Think Barter

In conversation with Jo Stumpf:

Steps: *"You seem to have a very creative approach to doing business. Can you give us some examples of your ideas?"*

Stumpf: *"The idea is to generate the maximum result for the minimum risk and cost. For instance, could I go to my chiropractor and ask him or her to put my flyer into their mailing package? Or how about sending change-of-address cards on behalf of someone who's just bought one of my houses?"*

As Jo Stumpf notes, the ideal situation is to produce the greatest result for the smallest expenditure of time and money. One of the best ways to accomplish this is to think in terms of exchanging favours with people whose needs may complement yours.

Who are some of the people who have you as their client? Your children's orthodontist, the manager of your health club, the salesperson from whom you recently purchased a piano… make a list of all such people, and think about how you can serve each other's needs without causing them undue inconvenience. This last point is important. Most people will be pleased to enter into a bartering agreement, but not if it's a bother to them.

Here's another idea that Jo came up with; Let's say you've just bought a house from him, and he referred you to a furniture store where you purchased $10,000 worth of goods. He would then go to the furniture store and ask them to write a letter on his behalf to everyone they know. In exchange, he would continue to refer all his clients to them. The result? More clients for Jo, and more clients for the furniture store. The same idea can be applied to carpet cleaners, renovation contractors, or any other business associated with the needs of new home buyers.

Step 2: Don't Do What the Average Guy Is Doing

In conversation with Marilyn Jennings:

Steps: *"You didn't always produce as much as you do today. What's different now?"*

Jennings: *"I spent 14 years working the way the industry teaches you do it. All the wrong things. And then I came across a business article that turned my thinking around. It said that if you want to be average, do what everyone else in your business is doing, and if you want to be successful do the opposite."*

Steps: *"So what you are saying, basically, is that you have to be unique and different."*

Jennings: *"Yes, my theory is to do the opposite. Everything in our society is geared to make you look average, so doing the opposite allows you to be above average. Certainly it has made all the difference for me and my business."*

Many entrepreneurs persist in believing they can soar to success on the back of a lemming. When considered thoughtfully, it is self-evident that if you use average strategies, you will get average results. In order to achieve outstanding results, you have to throw away much of the "wisdom" that has been handed down to you about your field of business. You have to do your own experimenting—which may include trying things that are "known" not to work—and come to your own conclusions.

For instance, one of the no-nos in real estate sales is knocking on doors. Because it was the opposite of what everyone else was doing, Marilyn Jennings decided to try this route when she arrived in Calgary. She set herself the goal of looking at 20 to 30 houses and knocking on 50 doors per day. *Every* day. She calls it "getting out of her comfort zone." Fear of door-knocking, she insists, is a paper tiger that people build up in their own minds. The only way around such a fear is to force yourself to act in spite of it. Eventually, the dreaded activity will lose its sting and may even become enjoyable.

The result of Marilyn's original and systematic approach was that after one year in Calgary—a city of 700,000 where she knew nobody when she arrived—her net earnings from commissions were neatly above her target of $100,000.

 # Step 3 — *Give Your Enterprise a Personality*

In conversation with Alex Tilley:

Steps: *"I'm standing here outside your store, and I see... a gigantic moose. Can you tell me what that's all about?"*

Tilley: *"What I'm trying to do is amuse people. Basically this is my place, and I have the right as the owner to do whatever I feel like out here. And it so happens that what I feel like doing, a lot of people enjoy seeing."*

Creating an image is not exclusive to retail stores. Image is conveyed through business cards, letterhead, waiting rooms, private offices, company brochures, telephone manner, and invoices, to name a few. If your business looks and sounds like all the others, you will be regarded as one of the pack. While this doesn't mean you won't get any clients, there is something to be gained by creating your own personality.

Humour always works, as Alex Tilley's example shows. An oversized moose puts a smile on people's faces. If customers inquire about it, his staff can tell them that it is a 16-foot Easter Island model weighing about 16,000 pounds. In the inside of his store, there is a replica of a cave wall in France, complete with drawings and paintings. In addition to being creative and memorable, this display reinforces the high-adventure theme that links all Alex's products.

Another example of creative image building is a small Italian restaurant in Toronto, where Italian restaurants number in the thousands and are often hard to tell apart. Instead of erecting the usual neon sign with the restaurant's name on it, the owners commissioned a sculptor to create a giant and very realistic-looking nose with a hook and flared nostrils. The name of the restaurant is nowhere to be seen. In fact, the only way you can learn it is by word of mouth. This makes frequenters feel like insiders, and, along with the nose and fine home-style cuisine, has given the unassuming little restaurant a reputation as one of the "in" places to dine.

Step 4 Get an Angle

In conversation with Ed Mirvish:

Steps: *"A lot of people have tried to imitate your Honest Ed's store, but haven't really succeeded. What do you think accounts for that?"*

Mirvish: *"My basic philosophy is keep it simple, fulfill a need, go against the trend, and get an angle."*

Steps: *"What is your angle?"*

Mirvish: *"Here at Honest Ed's we have a policy of no service. When you walk into the store, the first sign you see is, 'Don't bother our help, they have their own problems.' "*

When starting out in business, the tendency is to try to be all things to all people. The extreme form of this tendency can be seen in business cards (most commonly seen in rural areas) that read, "Roofing, Parcel Delivery, Landscaping, and Tax Returns."

Chances are, you will do better by figuring out an angle— preferably a unique one that nobody else has thought of—and sticking to it. Your potential client base may be smaller, but there will be a much better fit between your service and the needs of those clients. If you try to please everybody, you will have little or no appeal to a theoretically broad client base, which in practice doesn't amount to much.

Ed Mirvish has a strong angle for Honest Ed's—providing no service, and passing on the resulting cost savings to the customers.

He delivers this message with humour and clarity, so that customers know exactly what to expect. A Jewish deli in Montreal has fashioned its image around the same concept of bare-bones service. The restaurant has acquired a reputation for the charming rudeness of its staff, and customers line up for the privilege of being rushed through their meal and shooed out as they're swallowing their last mouthful of smoked meat.

A creative angle means that your business is different and memorable, and attracts repeat customers whose needs correspond exactly to what you're offering.

 # Step 5: Set Your Products Apart With Original Features

In conversation with Alex Tilley:

Steps: *"Describe your clothing. What makes it so distinctive?"*

Tilley: *"Number one, it has to be functional, it has to do the job. It also has to be good-looking. It's got to have that 'curb appeal,' as they say in real estate; otherwise you won't buy it. But beyond good looks and high quality, our products tend to have unique and innovative features that set them apart. It's a question of creative craftsmanship."*

In today's cutthroat business arena, it is more important than ever to stand out from the crowd. It is also more difficult, since everyone in the crowd is playing the same game of trying to be different. In this sort of market, you have to dig deep into your creative resources if you want to get noticed.

If you've lived in the same neighbourhood for a while, you've probably seen many instances of a small business (such as a restaurant, video store or retail clothing outlet) closing shop only a few months after it opened. In many cases, the quality of the product was high, the prices were reasonable, the service competent, and the neighbourhood appropriate for that kind of business. So what happened? A likely possibility is that the "new kid on the block" didn't have anything to distinguish it from umpteen other establishments. So people had no reason to venture away from the stores and eateries they normally frequented.

Recognizing the importance of setting himself apart from the competition, Alex Tilley loads his products with features that nobody else has ever thought of. For example, his travel pants include secret pockets for passports, and other special compartments where people can keep their valuables. He uses only the strongest threads for these pockets, and reinforces them several times—"over-engineers," as he puts it. The result is a feature that is both creative and reliable—a powerful combination.

Step 6 — *Provide Unique Add-On Services*

In conversation with Alex Tilley:

Steps: *"In your store I saw a computer database of some sort. What was it?"*

Tilley: *"It's a travel advisory service, and it's free."*

Steps: *"Why have a travel advisory service in a clothing store?"*

Tilley: *"These days, service is the name of the game. And if we can come up with a useful and original service that's somehow related to our products, we get noticed."*

The day is rapidly approaching—indeed, some say it has already arrived—when it will no longer be sufficient for a clothing retailer to sell clothes, a video outlet to sell videos, or a stationery store to sell stationery. Add-on services, such as newsletters or databases, will become integral to the retail business. Computer and video technology is tailor-made for such services.

The custom-designed travel advisory service provided by Tilley's stores contains practical information about specific destinations at specific times of the year. If you are going to Bali on October 16, for instance, the service will tell you everything you need to know about Bali at that time—weather, customs, national holidays, health concerns, along with various do's and don'ts. With about 25 categories in all, the service is a big hit with customers.

To take another example, let's suppose you're a retailer selling in-line skating equipment. An interesting add-on service might be to provide a series of instructional videos—which you can either purchase or have specially made for you—about the sport. You can have shortened versions of the videos playing in the store, and rent out the full-length versions to customers. For people who buy a pair of in-line skates, rentals would be free.

The question to ask yourself when designing an add-on service is, "Will this service motivate customers to return to my place of business?" If you think the answer is yes, then give it a try. You don't have too much to lose, and what you stand to gain is an enthusiastic and loyal clientele.

Step 7: Use "Controlled Outrageousness"

In conversation with Jerry Wilson:

Steps: *"In your book, I came across the term 'controlled outrageousness'. It made me smile, but I wasn't sure what it meant."*

Wilson: *"Outrageous means silly or daring, and controlled means within the bounds of good taste."*

Steps: *"How does this apply to your marketing?"*

Wilson: *"It means I'm going to do some things that are pretty bizzarre but hopefully don't offend the client—that's where the 'controlled' part comes in."*

Times are not good for sensible people, according to Jerry Wilson. If you're used to doing things by the book, you may be in trouble. The good news is that you can be more creative than ever in the way you publicize, market, and transact your business. There is no such thing as inappropriate or too outrageous, Jerry believes, as long you stay more or less within the bounds of good taste. When promoting his own services, Jerry always tries to come up with things that will "keep customers on the edge of their seats."

For example, in order to highlight the idea of word-of-mouth marketing to his clients, he sent them each a set of those plastic teeth that can be wound up and sent bouncing across a desk. People have a lot of fun with them, and their message is clear: keep on chatting about Jerry's business, keep spreading the word. "What's important about the teeth," Jerry says, "is that when you see them you've got to play with them, no matter who you are. You can be 98 years old and you'll still want to play with them because they scream, *pick me up*! That reminds my customers to think about me, much more than a business card or even a glossy brochure. And they usually call me back laughing."

Step 8: Appeal to the Local Culture

In conversation with Arthur Fettig:

Steps: *"Do you vary your speeches depending on the type of audience and setting?"*

Fettig: *"I try to customize my jokes to each audience. One way of doing that is by knowing about the local culture."*

Steps: *"How does one go about finding out about the local culture?"*

Fettig: *"Well, you can read the papers for recent important information. A lot of it is common sense— people's concerns will depend on whether they live in a warm or cold climate, small town or big city, what kind of industries are located in their region, to name a few."*

Trotting out a canned speech without regard to the particularities of the audience you are dealing with is not very creative, says Arthur Fettig. Experience has confirmed his belief that "An audience responds most warmly if they feel you are concerned with them personally."

He once gave a speech in Newfoundland, for instance, where the controversy surrounding deforestation is a major local concern. So he opened his speech with the Sahara joke, which goes something like this: There was a fellow trying to get a job cutting trees in Newfoundland. The locals asked him what experience he had. He said he'd cut millions and millions of trees in the Sahara Forest. "You mean Sahara desert, don't you," the locals exclaimed. "It is now," he countered. Arthur says that the audience loved the joke, relaxed immediately, and was prepared to take in the rest of his speech with an attitude of openness and trust.

Perhaps out of laziness and perhaps out of reluctance to spend the extra money, advertisers and promoters often create generic material that doesn't reflect the local culture. In many cases, however, it is possible to customize your material with a minimum of effort and expenditure. If, for instance, you're putting together a product catalogue that is to be distributed nationally, it is easy to customize the inside front cover to reflect different geographical regions, such as Eastern, Central and Western.. You can do this through a photo, through the editorial, or both. The effect is a more intimate connection with the reader, which is usually well worth the small extra cost.

Step 9: Engage in Synergistic Activities

In conversation with Ed Mirvish:

Mirvish: *"I never wanted to be in the restaurant business."*

Steps: *"Well, that makes my next question pretty easy. Why did you go into it?"*

Mirvish: *"Once I had acquired the Royal Alexandra Theatre, it was so desolate that I thought if I opened a restaurant, each would complement the other."*

The term "synergistic" has become a buzzword in today's business parlance. The Oxford dictionary defines the word as referring to interactions whose "combined effect exceeds the sum of their individual effects." For instance, if one tablet each of pain-killer A and pain-killer B reduces your headache more effectively than either two tablets of A or two tablets of B, then the pharmaceutical products A and B are said to have a synergistic interaction.

In starting a restaurant in the vicinity of the Royal Alexandra theatre, Ed Mirvish's thinking was that the Royal Alex would boost sales in his restaurant, and vice versa. This is in fact what happened, even though everybody told him he was "crazy" to think he could open a 192-seat restaurant serving only roast beef. Ed's double venture turned out to be a classic case of synergy.

If you are doing more than one type of work in your business, ask yourself whether your activities are synergistic or unrelated, or even worse, antagonistic. (In this context, "antagonistic" means that doing activities A and B reduces your total volume of business as compared to doing only A or only B.) Ideally, you should pare down your business activities to those which complement and reinforce each other. If you are running a beauty salon, for instance, wig rentals are probably a more synergistic sideline than tanning beds.

Section 5

Communication

The Art of Connecting

Step 1: Find Out How You Can Help

In conversation with Bob Burg:

Steps: *"What are some of the secrets of effective networking?"*

Burg: *"Well, one thing you shouldn't be doing is simply going to these networking functions and handing out your business card to a hundred different people. Many people do this, never establish any relationships, and then they say, 'I tried networking and it didn't work.'"*

Steps: *"So what's the alternative?"*

Burg: *"Instead of being so focused on how the other person can be of use to you, find out how you can be of use to them."*

If you want to set yourself apart from the crowd at a fundraising luncheon, association meeting or networking function, try focusing on the needs of your conversation partners rather than on your own. Find out what you can do for them. Bob Burg advises ending a conversation with a question like, "How can I know if someone I'm talking to would be a good prospect for you?" He also suggests introducing your contacts to each other if you think the introduction would be beneficial to them, a practice he calls "positioning yourself as the Big Person on Campus."

On one level, it's the old you-scratch-my-back-and-I'll-scratch-yours principle: if you refer business to someone, that person will eventually refer business to you. But it's more than that. By showing an interest in helping other people, you are developing an attitude that will earn you respect—not to mention self-respect—in the business world.

And as an alternative to thrusting your business card at people at the first opportunity, Bob suggests asking them for their business cards, which in all likelihood will prompt them to ask for yours. Here again, the idea is to show interest in what they are doing.

Step 2: Develop the Art of Listening

In conversation with Hugh Rennie:

Steps: *"You've said you're interested in the less obvious aspects of communication. Can you give an example of one of these aspects?"*

Rennie: *"Yes. Most people think communication is about talking. I place a far greater value on listening than on talking. Of course, I'm not talking about any old kind of listening. It has to be active."*

At the heart of good communication is the ability to listen— truly listen—to what the other person is saying.

As Hugh Rennie points out, it is not enough simply to take in what is being said to you. As any psychiatrist will tell you, active listening, as opposed to passive listening, takes great concentration. One way to assess your listening skills is by the kinds of questions you ask. Are they relevant? Do they encourage further elaboration, or simply "yes" and "no" answers? Do they broaden the scope of the conversation? Hugh is fond of quoting the following statement from the French author Voltaire: "You can measure a person by the questions they ask, not by the answers they give."

If your conversation partner is talking about how new customs regulations have hampered his overseas operations, for instance, a pertinent question might be, "At what point in the bureaucratic process do the snags usually occur?" or, "With these new regulations in place, do you still consider it worthwhile to tap into the overseas market?" The first question leads the speaker to provide more specific detail, and the second encourages him to give general opinions that can be of value to other businesses, such as yours. Both questions convey interest, and make the speaker feel that his opinion is valued.

Step 3: Ask "Feel Good" Questions

In conversation with Bob Burg:

Steps: *"You've stressed the importance of asking questions when trying to establish a relationship with someone. What types of questions do you ask people?"*

Burg: *"I ask open-ended questions, what I call 'feel good' questions."*

Steps: *"By which you mean ...?"*

Burg: *"Questions that are designed to keep the person talking."*

Though few would care to admit it, most people love to talk about themselves. More specifically, they love to talk about their pet projects, their aspirations, and their past successes. So if you ask people questions that enable them to carry on about these topics, they will feel good about the conversation, and by extension, about you. One of the questions Bob Burg says is almost guaranteed to make the other person feel good is, "How did you get started in the (fill in the blank) business?" Another is, "What do you enjoy most about your work?"

Of course, it's not a simple matter of firing off questions. You have to be genuinely interested in hearing the answers, or else people will sense your falseness even if they can't put their finger on it. So what do you do if someone is boring you to tears? Either excuse yourself and find another conversation partner, or challenge yourself to come up with more interesting questions.

For instance, rather than asking someone to list their major contracts, you could ask them about their most unusual or unlikely client, or about an off-beat marketing idea that was more effective than expected. Such questions are not only more interesting but also more useful to you.

Step 4: Use Words and Ideas People Can Understand

In conversation with Hugh Rennie:

Steps: *"You're known as a man who doesn't mince words."*

Rennie: *"In my tapes, I show people how to 'Cut the bullshit and get to the point.' That's the actual wording I use."*

Steps: *"Specifically, how does one accomplish this?"*

Rennie: *"Write like you talk. Use short words and short sentences. Hit people with an idea, and develop it."*

Have you ever gotten a sinking feeling when leafing through a legal document, tax form, or computer manual, knowing that the language is likely to be heavy or obscure or simply confusing? Many of us have had that experience, but forget about simplicity when we're on the transmitting end. A part of us still believes that wielding complicated words will impress people. Even if this were true, however, it wouldn't accomplish what we want, which is to have people understand our ideas and feel comfortable in our presence.

There is nothing wrong with using specialized words when the occasion calls for it, such as a keynote speech at a professional association where everybody uses the same lingo. More important than the words you use is the way you put them together. Your sentences should be clear, easy to follow, and arranged in a logical sequence of ideas. Albert Einstein believed that no matter how complex the subject, a good explanation should be understandable to a five-year-old.

Hugh Rennie's maxim of "writing like you talk" does not mean you should be sloppy with your grammar, as people often are when speaking off the cuff. Rather, it means you should retain the simplicity, freshness and casual style of spoken conversation in your writing. If you have a main point to make, cut right to the chase. Don't hide behind clichés or vague generalizations such as "In this post-industrial society, businesses have to keep up to date with changing technology in order to stay ahead of the competition." Such statements are obvious but non-specific—they provide the listener with *no* useful information. And if it isn't useful, why say it at all?

 **Step 5** *Don't Prepare Too Rigidly*

In conversation with Peter Urs Bender:

Steps: *"Is there such a thing as being 'too prepared' when giving a presentation?"*

Urs Bender: *"If by 'prepared' you mean knowing your stuff, then the answer is no. But there is such a thing as over-memorizing."*

Steps: *"You mean, memorizing your speech word for word?"*

Urs Bender: *"Yes. It's a dangerous practice—it makes you lose the ability to think on your feet."*

In business, as in everything else, it's important to have a certain amount of flexibility in your behaviour. You should be able to fine-tune your actions in response to the feedback you're getting from your surroundings. If you're giving a talk, for example, and you don't seem to be connecting with your audience, you should be able to make adjustments in your delivery—to inject more or less humour, to raise or lower your voice, to speak more quickly or more slowly—in response to your audience.

If you memorize your presentation word-for-word, you run the risk of being locked into a groove. Your mind is in an automatic rather than a creative mode, and those unexpected flashes of insight are less likely to pop into your head. You are also less able to adjust your style. Another risk of over-memorizing is having a memory blank and being unable to ad-lib around it.

Peter Urs Bender uses cue cards for his presentations, and "never more than seven." More than this number, he says, and you run the risk of being too committed to a particular sequence. On each card, he writes up to five key words. Each word is the kernel of a thought or anecdote. Interestingly, he writes the words in different colours. A red word tells him that the point needs to be emphasized strongly, while a blue word is a signal to tread softly. He also draws pictures, such as smiling faces, to remind him to smile at his audience.

Peter believes that giving presentations is both an art and a science. The more intelligently you prepare (this is the science part), the more likely your talk will be a work of art.

Step 6 — Alternate Seriousness With Humour

In conversation with Arthur Fettig:

Steps: *"When you are delivering the meat, so to speak, of a speech, do you use humour at that point, or do you just convey a strong, serious message?"*

Fettig: *"Laughter is a good change for an audience. It's physical, it gets them moving—leaning forward in their chairs, throwing back their heads, and all the things we do when we laugh. Movement is a tool to keep them listening."*

Some public speakers prefer to start with a joke, others say it's better to plunge right into the heart of the matter. But virtually all speakers agree that a good speech has to have both humour and seriousness in it. Too much seriousness, and the audience gets depressed or uncomfortable. Too much humour, and the audience feels cheated of substance.

The same principle can be applied to any form of communication, whether spoken or written. For instance, if you're sending a company CV to an executive, you will make a more vivid impression if you include some humour in your cover letter. (Example: "Empty promises are like a frosty beer mug with apple cider inside it.") If, on the other hand, there is nothing but humour in your letter, you run the risk of not being regarded as a professional.

In addition to being a welcome change in a serious presentation, humour releases tension. "I learned from studying Shakespeare that dramatic tension must periodically be released with humour,"

Arthur says. "You carry people along in a drama, then use humour to release the tension, then carry them along further, then release it again, then take them still further, and so on." If you don't allow for this periodic release, you will end up overwhelming or alienating people, and losing their attention as a result.

Step 7 Avoid Hackneyed Phrases

In conversation with Alex Tilley:

Steps: *"You've said that one of the secrets of your success is that you care so much. How do you convey this feeling to your customers?"*

Tilley: *"In the way we talk, for one thing. Instead of using the usual hackneyed phrases, our staff is trained to use words that communicate caring."*

Stay away from the trite phrases that have become meaningless through overuse, Alex Tilley cautions. As an example of such a phrase, he mentions the automatic "Can I help you?" that most salespeople use as an opening line. Shoppers in search of a specific item will probably tell you what they're looking for in response to that question, but people who are simply browsing will likely give you the knee-jerk response of "I'm just looking." The result is that no real communication has taken place.

Alex's salesclerks are instructed never to say "Can I help you?" Instead, they greet customers with an warm, friendly opener such as "Welcome to Tilley's, have a cookie, and can I get you a coffee?" This, says Alex, is language that shows caring without putting any pressure on the shopper. The result is that, whether a shopper ends up buying something or not at that particular time, he or she will feel welcome and well taken care of, and will likely make further visits to the store.

Alex says that if he were in another type of business, such as real estate, he would apply the same principle of avoiding or altering the conversational clichés of the industry. For example, instead of simply telling a client that he had a great house for them to see, he would ask, "Can I show you something unusual about this house?" Few people could refuse an offer like that, he guesses.

 # Step 8 — *Use the Power of Touch*

In conversation with Arthur Fettig:

Fettig: *"I go out to the audience and touch people's hands. I think that physically touching someone, even shaking hands, is a very personal and very effective way of communicating."*

Steps: *"You aren't worried that physical contact might be considered too forward?"*

Fettig: *"You have to be sensitive, of course. But if you touch someone with sincerity, perhaps while looking at them in the eye and saying 'thank you for being here,' they tend to respond very positively."*

Arthur Fettig believes that touch is contagious. If you touch one person in an audience, many of the people sitting around that person may also feel as though they've been touched. Arthur has lectured in amphitheatres seating several thousand, and people in the back row have sometimes told him that they could actually feel him touching them and shaking their hands, even though he hadn't literally done that.

Of course, it goes without saying that any touching has to be done with restraint and respect, particularly in male-female interactions where meanings can easily be misinterpreted. And if you are alone with somebody, regardless of their sex, it is never a good idea to touch that person.

In a highly public situation, such as a lecture or networking meeting, touch can go a long way toward easing tension and breaking down walls between people. In his own presentations, Arthur favours touching hands, which he feels carries no threat to most people. At an appropriate time during a lecture, he might go up to somebody, touch his or her hand, and say something like, "My job is to touch one of you tonight and change part of your outlook on life. If I can do that, I consider the evening a success."

Arthur cautions against touching people robotically, without regard for their reaction. If you antagonize one person, he warns, you're likely to antagonize the whole audience. Sensitivity—continually gauging the response you're getting and adjusting your style if necessary—is the essence of being a good communicator, and especially important when using touch as a form of communication.

 # Step 9
Be Selective About How You Use Your Breath

In conversation with Bob Burg:

Steps: *"When I think of networking, I think of going to the chamber of commerce, for example, and mingling with as many people as possible."*

Burg: *"Well, that's the usual idea—you know, mingle mingle mingle and then go home. As far as I'm concerned, that doesn't necessarily accomplish the purpose you want."*

Steps: *"What does, then?"*

Burg: *"In a nutshell, spending more time with fewer people—being selective about how you use your breath."*

If you've just written the great Canadian novel and are trying to get it published, it doesn't make sense to send it out to publishers who specialize in non-fiction or in children's stories. You'll not only waste your time, stationery and stamps, but your morale will sink as the standardized rejection letters roll in.

The same logic applies to networking, of course. If you go to a networking function and engage in a frenzy of information-swapping, you can tell yourself that you've accomplished something. In the short term, you feel energized. But then, over the months, you have to face the reality that none of these "contacts" is of any use to you.

Bob Burg suggests targeting four or five people at a networking function, and spending 10 to 15 minutes with each. You can then go home with the sense of having *really* accomplished something. And how do you target those people? Ask yourself the simple question, "How likely is it that this person, or the people in this person's sphere of influence, will require my product or service in the foreseeable future?" If you're selling educational software, for instance, go for the department store executive or school principal and ignore the financial consultant.

Sometimes the answer will only come to you after you've spent a couple of minutes chatting with someone. If the answer is no, then excuse yourself politely at the first opportunity and move on to the next person.

Step 10: Don't Send "I-Oriented" Messages

In conversation with Bob Burg:

Steps: *"So you've done your networking, you go home, and wait for the calls. Right?"*

Burg: *"Well, not quite. If you've followed the steps correctly, you probably have about four or five cards from people with whom you'd like to pursue a relationship. So the first thing I would do is send them a little thank-you note."*

Steps: *"What should it say in the note?"*

Burg: *"Whatever you do, don't send an 'I-oriented' message."*

While it's important—indeed, essential—that you follow up on the contacts you make at a business gathering, the mere act of sending a note isn't enough. Like everything else you do in the business world, this step has to be done right in order to be effective. And one of the wrong ways to do it is to give what Bob Burg calls an "I-oriented" message. For instance, if you're a real-estate broker, an I-oriented message would be, "If you ever need to buy a home, please call me." All that does, according to Bob, is show the recipient that you're "nothing more than everyone else." In other words, it accomplishes nothing.

Here's how Bob does it: He uses an 8-1/2" by 3-1/2" post-card note, which fits nicely into a regular business envelope. His company logo is printed on the right side of the postcard, along with contact information and a small, classy-looking headshot of himself. He handwrites the note in blue ink, keeping it simple and "you-oriented." Typically it's something like, "Dear Gary, thank you for letting me have the pleasure of meeting you. If I can ever refer business your way, I certainly will." And he always hand-stamps the envelope.

It may sound like a lot of effort for someone you hardly know, but the result is someone who feels good about you and would like to help you—as Bob puts it, one of your "walking ambassadors."

 # Step 11   *Customize Your Approach*

In conversation with Jerry Wilson:

Steps: *"You've talked earlier about bombarding your clients with reminders of your presence. I'm interested to know if you use this approach with all your clients."*

Wilson: *"While my general philosophy is to keep reminding people of my existence, of course I tailor the specifics to each individual client."*

Steps: *"So what exactly do you vary?"*

Wilson: *"Some clients might be happy to hear from me every week, others might not care for that at all. You have to have a feel for that sort of thing or you're in trouble."*

Have you ever walked into a clothing store and been practically assaulted by a salesclerk who seemed oblivious to your wish to be left alone to browse? Have you ever tried to get information about a house from an agent who was concentrating so hard on selling you the house that he or she couldn't "hear" your questions? Have you ever requested that you be crossed off a mailing list, or that a supplier not contact you for a certain period of time, only to have your request ignored?

A large part of business is human relations, and a large part of human relations is sensitivity. A businessperson has to be able to read people's verbal and non-verbal signals, and react accordingly.

While Jerry Wilson's style of self-promotion is on the aggressive side, he is keenly aware of when to back off. He calls this "knowing the basics."

To return to the clothing store example, some customers love to have a salesperson give them advice, show them various outfits, and comment on how things look on them; other customers find it unnecessary and annoying to have a salesclerk hovering over them and "helping" them find sizes they are perfectly capable of getting themselves.

There is no single sequence of words and behaviours that can be applied to every customer. When it comes to communications, one size definitely doesn't fit all.

Step 12: Upgrade Your Persuasion Skills

In conversation with Hugh Rennie:

Steps: *"You're known to be a highly persuasive person. Is it really so important for an entrepreneur to have this skill?"*

Rennie: *"It's not the best idea that beats the competition. It's the best-presented idea. This may seem unfair, but I look upon it as a challenge."*

No matter how brilliant your business idea or how spectacular the quality of your work, if you don't know how to convince other people of your talents, they will remain "in the bottom drawer," as it were. As Hugh Rennie points out, it is not productive to decry the unfairness of a world which sometimes rewards salesmanship over skill. To do be truly successful in business, you have to have both.

A persuasive person need not be aggressive or even particularly outgoing. If your personality is more retiring, you can still develop the ability to win people over within the framework of your own style. According to Hugh, it is certainly not by the quantity or loudness of your words that you become a persuasive person. Instead, it is by the way you present yourself through your tone and your body language.

Bob encourages people to tape themselves while giving a fictitious sales presentation. Although you may feel a little foolish at first, you will probably make some useful discoveries. Try to emulate the way you would sound in a real-life situation. When playing back the tape, put yourself in a client's shoes. Are you convinced or bored, charmed or intimidated, by what you are hearing? Do you repeat yourself unnecessarily? Do you clear your throat excessively? Do you let your sentences trail off vaguely? Or conversely, do you sound too forceful, perhaps even pushy? Repeat the exercise a day or two later, drawing on the insights you gained by listening to the first run-through.

Like all talents, the art of persuasion is a combination of natural ability and practice. Not a problem, says Hugh: if your natural ability is not very high, you'll simply need more practice.

Section 6

Steps Ahead

Toward a Successful Future

 *Expand Your Sphere of Influence*

In conversation with Bob Burg:

Steps: *"What do you mean by the term 'sphere of influence'?"*

Burg: *"Each and every one of us knows about 250 people naturally in our lives. That's what I call our personal sphere of influence."*

Steps: *"And how do you put that to use in your business life?"*

Burg: *"Every time you come into contact with someone, you can figure that this person also knows about 250 people. And each of those people knows 250 more. So you can see that the potential for making connections is limitless."*

The theory is simple but mind-boggling: according to Bob Burg, everybody—even Mr. Joe Average—has a personal sphere of influence of about 250 people. So for every contact you make, you have the potential to tap into 250 more. If you make twenty contacts, that's a potential 5,000 people in your sphere of influence. And if you consider the 250 people associated with each of those 5,000 people, you have a total of 1,250,000 people within your sphere! Obviously it's not that simple in practice. In order to tap into someone else's sphere of influence, you have to be successful in establishing a rapport with that person.

To start with, make a list of the 250 people in your personal sphere. They include relatives and friends, business associates, doctors, lawyers, shopkeepers, financial advisors, your child's teacher or soccer coach, members of your congregation or volunteer association, and the man you sometimes run into while walking your dog. Be creative, and challenge yourself to come up with a written list of at least 250 people who are currently in your life.

Step 2: Devote Time to Building Relationships

In conversation with Peter Oliver:

Steps: *"Aside from the personal satisfaction it has given you, has fundraising been helpful to your business?"*

Oliver: *"Most definitely. I found that the profile of our business increased dramatically when I got involved in fundraising."*

Steps: *"And how did this translate into getting more business?"*

Oliver: *"Fundraising helps you meet people, which is the first step in building relationships, which eventually leads to more business. Our goal is to have a relationship with the top one-hundred companies in Toronto."*

The equation is simple: today's contacts are tomorrow's clients.

While "cold" strategies can and do sometimes lead to business transactions, in the long term, there is no substitute for building a network of personal and business contacts. It is human nature to prefer doing business with "known quantities." If you are diligent about cultivating and maintaining relationships, you can count on the fact that some of these people will eventually require your product or service.

Peter Oliver's primary motivation for getting involved in fundraising was that his daughter has diabetes, and he wanted to raise money for the Juvenile Diabetic Foundation. But he is the first to acknowledge that he has also reaped business benefits from the venture, not the least of which is the opportunity to hold regular meetings with fifty senior executives from top companies in Toronto. When these executives need to book Christmas or mid-year functions for their companies, Oliver's restaurants are fresh on their minds.

It doesn't matter what approach you take to building relationships—fundraising is only one of them—it matters only that you do it with sincerity and consistency over the years.

Use Discrimination in Hiring

In conversation with Harry Rosen:

Steps: *"I'm sure you've been asked this question many times before, but could you tell me something about what makes your stores unique?"*

Rosen: *"At one point, I realized that I had to sell not only to the consumer but also to my staff. The people who work for us have to be committed to our ideas and principles. Of course, it helps to hire people who can relate to those principles in the first place."*

Steps: *"So hiring suitable people is a key factor, you would say?"*

Rosen: *"Yes. There is nothing more inefficient than constantly hiring and firing. I'm amazed at how often this occurs in business."*

Hiring the wrong person for a job is one of the costliest mistakes in business. Finding and training a replacement (not to mention severance payments) is a huge drain on your time and your money.

What makes someone appropriate for a position? According to Harry Rosen, there does not need to a perfect match between a candidate's experience and the job they are being hired for. It is much easier to learn a new software package than to learn a personality. Employers seem to have a better understanding of this principle in Japan, where interviews tend to focus more on personality and working style than on precisely matching experience. If you require a gregarious person for a job, make sure that is what you're getting. Conversely, if you need someone who will be working alone for long periods of time, take care to evaluate all candidates from this point of view. It is not enough to ask someone to describe their own personality type, because candidates will often try to give you what they perceive to be the "right" answer. You must observe and judge for yourself. And when checking someone's references, don't divulge too much about the position you're trying to fill or the traits you're looking for. Ask open-ended questions, such as "How would you describe Sally Sweet's working style?", that encourage the other person to talk honestly.

You also need to assess whether a candidate is too experienced for a position. While there is no such thing as an overly motivated employee, there is such a thing as over qualification. If your hunch is that someone will be bored after six months, listen to it. You want to hire a person who will be interested in and challenged by the position for a long period of time.

Just as important, according to Harry, is to select employees who believe in your product or service. Harry is on the lookout for people whose personal image resonates with that of his stores, which is classy and fairly conservative. He also seeks employees who have a genuine liking for his product, who will be able to identify with it, and who will take pride in representing it to the public.

 *Keep Your Employees Motivated and Accountable*

In conversation with Peter Oliver:

Oliver: *"We spend literally hundreds of dollars training our managers in goal programs."*

Steps: *"How does this benefit your business? Does it really make them more effective managers?"*

Oliver: *"In general terms, it motivates them to be a part of our vision. On a practical level, we help them decide what they want to accomplish, and we provide them with a set of action kits to help them get there. Most importantly, we give them feedback and make them accountable for their goals."*

Accountability, according to Peter Oliver, takes a certain amount of discipline. It is all too easy to set pie-in-the-sky budget objectives, for instance, and then forget about them when the reality begins to deviate from predictions. In order to get maximum productivity and respect from your staff, you will have to show them that your expectations are for real. You will also have to find ways to keep them motivated in the face of these high expectations.

Motivating your staff means doing simple things like sending them a thank-you note for a job well done. It means having a forum, such as a general meeting or suggestion box, where every employee can contribute his or her ideas. Above all, it means *listening* to people, no matter which rung they occupy on the ladder.

Accountability means that if you and an employee have both determined that a certain objective is reasonable, and then the employee fails to meet that objective, you will insist that he or she provide you with an explanation, along with strategies to close in on the objective in the future. In some cases, of course, the goal will have to be revised; in others, it will be wisest to either terminate or transfer the employee. True accountability is nothing more than fairness.

 # Step 5

Stay in Touch With Your Staff and Clients

In conversation with Harry Rosen:

Steps: *"Harry, you mentioned that you don't sit in an ivory tower and wait for an assistant to come and tell you what is happening down in the trenches."*

Rosen: *"That's right. You can have the most sophisticated reporting systems today, but sitting in your corner office and reading reports will only furnish you certain information. There are those down-to-earth questions that can't be answered by a computer."*

Steps: *"Such as?"*

Rosen: *"Such as how your staff is behaving towards customers, how customers are reacting to this or that technique. To get answers to these questions, you have to go down into the trenches."*

One thing hasn't changed with Harry Rosen's success: every Saturday, he can be found at one of his stores, selling clothes along with his staff. Over the years, he has worked behind the counter of each and every one of his stores in North America. Is this really necessary, one might ask?

Harry believes that it is, for several reasons. For one thing, morale is highest when employees know that the person at the helm isn't "too good for them," that he or she wants to stay connected with all levels of the operation. They can also learn by example, which is always more effective than simply following instructions. As Harry puts it, "It's a do-as-I-do rather than do-as-I-say situation."

Another benefit, as he points out, is that certain questions can be answered only by being there. Harry finds that by observing customers' habits—what degree of involvement they prefer from a salesperson, which sections of the store they are most drawn to, whether they are responding to special incentives such as a pre-Christmas sale bin—he can gain valuable information about how to serve them in the future.

 **Step 6** *Don't Rest on Your Laurels*

In conversation with Harry Rosen:

Steps: *"'Your reputation precedes you' is a phrase you must have heard often."*

Rosen: *"Reputation is not a static thing, though. You have to keep updating. You have to stay in touch with the forces of youth."*

Steps: *"Are you saying that young people aren't aware of your long-standing reputation?"*

Rosen: *"Whether aware or not, the current generation doesn't give much credit to past history. 'What have you done for me lately?' is the only question that concerns them."*

Like radioactive material, a reputation has a limited shelf-life, after which it becomes ineffectual. A typical scenario is of a company producing a breakthrough product, acquiring a reputation, selling briskly for a few months or years, becoming complacent about its success, until another (usually smaller) company sneaks up with a product line that completely outclasses the first one.

Harry Rosen makes a distinction between his ideals, which haven't changed over the years, and his ideas, which he has had to change continually. While the tone of his stores is still on the conservative side, he has incorporated some of the more enduring fashion trends of the current generation, such as brighter colours and more casual looks, into his selection. Had he assumed that business would take care of itself once his reputation was established, he might not be around today.

"Consumers are your best guides," Harry advises. "They will tell you if they accept or reject your standards, and they will tell you what you should be doing today. But you also have to know when not to react to the consumer. It's a delicate balance."

Listen especially to the young consumer, is Harry's final word. "You need to be in touch with the vital forces of youth, which you have to completely attract in order to ensure your survival as a business."

Step 7: Don't Grow Beyond Your Level of Comfort

In conversation with Ed Mirvish:

Steps: *" You never really wanted to expand your businesses, did you?"*

Mirvish: *"What I did not want ever was to chain out."*

Steps: *"You must have considered it, though."*

Mirvish: *"I had several offers to start chains in the States and across Canada, but I never really considered them because I didn't think I would enjoy it. What I do is very personalized."*

The Peter principle states that employees in a corporation tend to rise to their level of incompetence. What holds true for individuals is also true for businesses. As soon as the bottom line starts looking good, business owners catch the expansion bug, thinking that more must be better. If more does indeed prove to be better, the business keeps on expanding until... things start taking a downhill turn.

So how is one to decide whether expansion is a wise move? While the success of an expansion plan cannot be predicted with any accuracy, certain types of ventures lend themselves better to expansion than others. In the case of a restaurant, for instance, it depends on what kind of establishment it is. If the place is quirky, trendy, or has a distinctive neighbourhood flavour, expansion can ruin its appeal, which is based on singularity. Other types of restaurants, such as donut shops, family-style eateries or the ubiquitous wood-stove pizza joints, can continue to thrive with several outlets.

In many cases, the size of a business doesn't make any difference in terms of net profit. Owners of consulting firms have often found that when they downsize, they get fewer billings but their profits stay about the same. In such a case, there is little to justify the hassle of a large operation.

Above all, you have to think of what expansion means to you psychologically. Your day-to-day concerns will shift from dealing with clients to administering a bureaucracy. If this is what you want, then go ahead with your expansion plan if you've determined that it is financially sound.

It wasn't what Ed Mirvish wanted. He preferred the idea of running a few separate businesses, each with its own personality. He knew this about himself, and is the happier for having listened to his intuition.

 # Step 8   *Don't Be a Prima Donna*

In conversation with Ed Mirvish:

Steps: *"I'd like to ask you a bit about your book."*

Mirvish: *"I wanted to write a book in my own words. After all these years you forget a lot, but when they said they were going to pay me, I remembered everything. I even remembered things that never happened."*

Steps: *"Did the publishers give you free rein?"*

Mirvish: *"Pretty much, except with the title. But they were paying for it, so I figured they could call it whatever they wanted."*

Ed Mirvish takes justifiable pride in having reached the top from a starting point of no money or education. Accordingly, he wanted the title of his book to highlight the contrast between then and now, and thought that "From Dundas Street to Buckingham Palace" was a good choice. But the publishers of his book decided on the title of "How to Build an Empire on an Orange Crate," which they presumably thought was snappier and more humorous. Ed might well have insisted on his own choice, and because of his stature, might have gotten his way. But he decided to let the matter drop, because it was more a question of personal preference than of artistic integrity.

There is a fine line between principle and preference, and only you can decide if a particular situation falls into the first or the second category. Insisting on having every detail going your way, just because you have the muscle to get what you want, is a misuse of your power. You will eventually acquire the reputation of being difficult to deal with, and might lose some business as a result. On the other hand, insisting on your principles (for example, demanding that racist or sexist slurs be removed from articles written about you) is behaving with integrity, which in the long run will earn you respect.

 # Step 9
Avoid the Tyranny of the Urgent

In conversation with Harold Taylor:

Steps: *"You talked about the tyranny of the urgent. Can you explain what you mean by that?"*

Taylor: *" There are those things that are urgent and important, and they have to be done right away. There are also things that are important but not urgent, which are being delayed while we work on a third category, the urgent but not important."*

Steps: *"How can something be urgent but not important?"*

Taylor: *"It's really an ironic phrase which means that I convince myself something is urgent even though I know deep down that it's not very important."*

We all play psychological tricks on ourselves, and Harold Taylor's "tyranny of the urgent" is one such trick. We convince ourselves that something unimportant is urgent because we want to appear busy and harried, both to others and to ourselves; because we want to avoid doing unpleasant but important things; or because we haven't developed the ability to step back and distinguish between things that need doing and things that simply fill time.

In the worst-case scenario, treating every task as a dire emergency can result in physical illness, as it did for Harold Taylor, who ended up being hospitalized for bleeding ulcers. The silver lining behind that cloud was that Harold was forced to reevaluate his way of doing business, and as a result, became a leading efficiency expert. But it shouldn't be necessary to wait until you get ill before learning to be selective about how you use your time and how you react to stress.

Stress, Harold believes, is something we create rather than something "out there" in the environment. Now, if someone calls and tells him that he has to be there in 15 minutes or he'll lose the job, he thinks, "Well, I may lose the job, but I won't lose my life or my family or my friends." This balanced attitude has not hampered his career—to the contrary, he is doing better than ever.

Step 10  Don't Sweat the Small Stuff

In conversation with Patricia Fripp:

Fripp: *"I'm one of the few people who actually enjoy many aspects of their business. I enjoy being in the office and doing office work, I enjoy meeting clients, I enjoy getting on a plane."*

Steps: *"Even when there's a two-hour delay in your flight?"*

Fripp: *"When I get on a plane—or even when I'm waiting for a delayed flight—I think, 'God just gave me five hours,' and so I enjoy that time too."*

Overdue invoices, lost purchase orders, clients who come down with the flu on the day you're supposed to close a deal with them... If you are an employee in a corporation, it is easier to take these annoyances in stride because your personal success isn't necessarily at stake. If you are running your own show, however, you are more likely to let life's inconveniences get to you.

Don't, says Patricia Fripp. In her own business life, she tries to adopt what she calls the Dolly Parton approach to inconvenience. She recalls seeing an interview with the actor Sally Field, who talked about how everybody was complaining during the filming of the movie *Steel Magnolias* because they had to wear thick clothes in intense heat; everybody, that is, except Dolly Parton. When someone commented to Dolly that she must be boiling in her heavy wig, Dolly answered that when she was young and poor, she wanted to grow up to be rich and famous, and promised herself that if she ever got what she wanted, she would not complain about anything.

If you find yourself focusing more on the inconvenience than on the joys of running your own business, it might be a good idea to remind yourself, as Dolly apparently does, that you've *chosen* this path because it's what you've always wanted to do.

Step 11 Keep a Sense of Humour

In conversation with Peter Oliver:

Steps: *"I'm looking at all the mottos posted on your wall. One of the things up there is humour."*

Oliver: *"We're all on this earth for a certain period of time, and you've got to enjoy yourself or else what's the point of it all? I ask my wife what she sees in me, and the first thing she says is a sense of humour."*

As Peter Oliver says, there's no point to anything—including success—if you don't enjoy it. Building an empire need not be a grim affair. If you've chosen a business that's right for you, and if you diligently apply all the principles that lead to success, then eventually you *will* get that success. Try to enjoy the steps along the way, and develop the ability to find humour in the small "tragedies" that befall your enterprise.

On a strictly business level, the benefit of having a sense of humour is that it is the most effective ice-breaker there is. The way Peter puts it, a sense of humour works because "people expect one thing, and then you give them another." That element of surprise can be the balance between closing and losing a deal.

Above all else, a sense of humour will be your personal rudder in the exciting and unpredictable waters of entrepreneurship. Here's hoping that your road to success is filled with many belly laughs!

FURTHER STEPS TO SUCCESS?

Don't hide your success in the closet—share it! If you or someone you know has a story, anecdote, poem or article to do with success, send it to us for consideration for a future volume of "Steps to Success."

Avi Rosen and Associates
32 Covewood Street
North York, Ontario M2M 2Z1 Canada
Tel: (416) 410-1314
Fax: (416) 221-7280

We appreciate your thoughtfulness. The author will receive credit for contributing.

Seminars, Workshops, Public Addresses

Avi Rosen and Associates offers a full range of services, including lectures, seminars, workshops, audio tapes, newsletters and other training aids. Contact us at the above address for further information.

Yours in success!
Avi Rosen

AVI ROSEN & ASSOCIATES
WE GET RESULTS!

Excerpts from letters to Avi Rosen concerning his educational offerings:

"You have written a book [Steps to Success] that belongs in no library. It belongs on every business, marketing and sales person's desk. Or night table. That way, he or she can refer to it continuously, for it is a real, honest-to-goodness necessity for constant reference for helping them ensure success in their field."

Jerry Goodis, Chairman
The Jerry Goodis Business Education Group, Inc.

"The fundamental information in your "Reference Guide 1995" is practical, easy to understand and an excellent reference document. It accurately reflects your extensive experience in this area of expertise."

Carl Fox, President
Toronto Real Estate Board

"Thank you for giving us the opportunity to hear your insight on enhancing our referral and networking skills. It was truly a pleasure to meet and talk with you."
Davendra Sankarlall, B.A.S., Associate Branch Sales Manager
Metropolitan Life

"Thank you for taking the time to meet with us today. We all enjoyed your presentation and will certainly be using your ideas for increasing our referral business."
L. Dianne Barber, Membership Director
The Fitness Institute

"The content of the [Listing and Selling Business Seminar] course I rate highly. It presented me with many more facts, documentation and methods that are more current and informative than I expected. You certainly presented them well."
Joseph Bosco, Associate Broker/Manager
W. Frank Real Estate Limited

STEP UP THE LADDER OF SUCCESS EVEN FURTHER WITH OUR SELECTION OF MULTIMEDIA TOOLS

If you found *Steps to Success* inspiring, you'll want to pursue your business dream with the passion and dedication of a winner. We can help you along that goal path with our selection of dynamic business tools. Just order from the form below or send for our free catalog of Tools of the Trade.

Buying and Selling Business	$35.00	_____
The Book of Real Estate Reference Forms	$59.95	_____
Fundamentals of Starting Your Own Business Brokerage Business Operations (video)	$25.00	_____
The Art of Starting Your Own Business (Audio and Video)	$35.00	_____
Fundamentals of Starting Your Own Retail Store (audio)	$25.00	_____
The Secrets of Starting Your Own Bakery Business (audio, video)	$25.00	_____
The Secrets of Starting Your Own Party Warehouse Business (audio and video)	$25.00	_____
Subtotal		_____
GST (Canadian residents add 7%)		_____
Shipping and handling ($3 per item)		_____
Total		_____

****

Name _____

Address _____

City/State or Province/Postal Code _____

Payment: Check_____ Money Order_____ MasterCard/Visa_____

MC/Visa Account #_____ Expiry Date:_____

Cardholder's Signature:_____

Add $3.00 shipping and handling for each item ordered. Canadian residents add 7% GST.